GOD AND ME

30 Sunday School Lessons to Cultivate a Relationship with God in Kids

by

Angela E. Powell

Copyright © 2019 Angela E. Powell

Unless otherwise indicated, all Scripture quotations are taken from the Holy Bible, New Living Translation, copyright © 1996, 2004, 2015 by Tyndale House Foundation. Used by permission of Tyndale House Publishers, Inc., Carol Stream, Illinois 60188. All rights reserved.

Scripture quotations marked MSG are taken from *THE MESSAGE*, copyright © 1993, 1994, 1995, 1996, 2000, 2001, 2002 by Eugene H. Peterson. Used by permission of NavPress. All rights reserved. Represented by Tyndale House Publishers, Inc.

All rights reserved. The purchase of this material entitles the buyer to reproduce activities and take home sheets for classroom use only – not for commercial resale. Reproduction of these materials for an entire school, church or district is prohibited. No part of this book may be reproduced (except as noted above), stored in a retrieval system, or transmitted in any form or by any means (mechanically, electronically, recording, etc.) without the prior written consent of Angela E. Powell.   Printed in the USA

ISBN-10: 0-9991594-3-7
ISBN-13: 978-0-9991594-3-9

TABLE OF CONTENTS

HOW TO USE THIS BOOK 5

UNIT 1: GOD HAS A PLAN FOR YOU AND ME 7
LESSON 1: CREATION OF THE WORLD 8
LESSON 2: CREATION OF MAN 16
LESSON 3: GOD'S PLAN FOR EVERYONE 21
LESSON 4: LIFE'S NOT FAIR BUT… 29
LESSON 5: GOD'S PLAN FOR ME 35

UNIT 2: GOD LOVES YOU AND ME 43
LESSON 1: WHAT IS LOVE? 44
LESSON 2: GOD LOOKS AT US WITH HEART EYES 51
LESSON 3: GOD'S LOVE NEVER CHANGES 61
LESSON 4: THE GOOD SAMARITAN 68
LESSON 5: ARE WE SHOWING GOD'S LOVE TO OTHERS? 75

UNIT 3: GOD SAVED YOU AND ME 81
LESSON 1: PALM SUNDAY – CELEBRATING JESUS 82
LESSON 2: THE LAST SUPPER – CELEBRATING PASSOVER 88
LESSON 3: THE GARDEN – JESUS PRAYS 93
LESSON 4: GOOD FRIDAY – JESUS DIES 99
LESSON 5: RESURRECTION SUNDAY – JESUS IS ALIVE! 105

UNIT 4: GOD MAKES YOU AND ME MIGHTY 113
LESSON 1: GOD GAVE QUEEN ESTHER COURAGE. 114
LESSON 2: GIDEON THE SCARED SOLDIER 121
LESSON 3: GOD RENEWS OUR STRENGTH 130
LESSON 4: GOD GIVES ME STRENGTH 136
LESSON 5: THE ARMOR OF GOD 143

UNIT 5: GOD CAN TALK TO YOU AND ME 150
LESSON 1: THE LORD'S PRAYER 151
LESSON 2: P.R.A.Y. PRAISE 157
LESSON 3: P.R.A.Y. REVEAL 162
LESSON 4: P.R.A.Y. ASSIST 168
LESSON 5: P.R.A.Y. YIELD 174

Angela E. Powell

TABLE OF CONTENTS

UNIT 6: GOD SENT THE HOLY SPIRIT TO YOU AND ME 180
LESSON 1: WHO IS THE HOLY SPRIT? 181
LESSON 2: THE HOLY SPIRIT IS LIKE FIRE 187
LESSON 3: THE HOLY SPIRIT IS LIKE WIND 192
LESSON 4: THE HOLY SPIRIT IS LIKE WATER 197
LESSON 5: THE HOLY SPIRIT IS LIKE A DOVE 202

REFERENCE 203

HOW TO USE THIS BOOK

Thank you for purchasing this book! I know the elementary aged kids in your church will have loads of fun experiencing these lessons with you. The lessons have been taught and tweaked over the course of a year with children ages 6 to 11. Below are some tips on using this curriculum.

TO BEGIN: I spent a lot of time researching how children in this age bracket learn before writing these lessons. As a result, I've tried to include hands-on activities or a way to engage some of the five senses, questions to help them process what they're being taught, and games that can be tied in and used as an object lesson. Many of the lessons are broken down into 5-10 minute sections. For example, the welcome can last five minutes, the game can last ten. The lessons are divided into 5-10 minute lecture sections with questions to ask, hands-on activities, games, and/or videos to divide up the time.

This book was designed for all churches and all budgets. Most, if not all of the items you need can be bought at a dollar store or donated from families in your church. It doesn't matter if your class has 1 or 50 children, you can use this book. There are options for everyone.

UNIT OVERVIEW

Each unit contains five lessons. The Overview Page shows the unit theme, a description of each lesson, and a link where you can find optional videos I've compiled for each unit.

THE LESSONS

SUPPLIES NEEDED: Each lesson starts with a list of supplies. These supplies will be shown with each section you'll use them in as well.

WELCOME: This section encourages children to get to know someone they don't know. Write the question on a white board before class starts. As children enter the class, encourage them to find someone new, or someone they don't know well to discuss the question with.

GAMES: Each lesson offers a game that ties into the scriptures being taught. As you play the game, use it to make a point about the lesson. Most of the games can be played with small or large groups by simply tweaking how the game is played. I offer suggestions on how to do this with most games.

LEARNING GOD'S WORD: Because children tend to have short attention spans, and because they learn by doing, many of the lessons have hands-on activities, and/or activities to engage their five senses so they stay connected with what is being taught. The important thing is to be

HOW TO USE THIS BOOK

excited about knowing God loves us and we can trust Him. When the teacher is enthusiastic about the lesson, the children will be drawn in.

MEMORY VERSE: There is one memory verse for each unit. Each lesson has a section that lets the kids practice the memory verse in class, but it will also be on their take home sheet so they can practice at home. Consider having a prize box as an incentive for kids to memorize scripture. One idea is to have the kids practice their verse all month and on the last Sunday, whoever can recite the verse without help can choose a prize.

PRAYER CIRCLES: This section is aimed at getting the kids comfortable with prayer and praying for one another. There are three methods in the book for teaching the kids how to hear God's voice. The lessons in the last two units focus entirely on hearing God's voice for themselves. The Reference section of this book will give you a little more detail about each method.

TAKE HOME SHEETS: There is a take home sheet at the end of each lesson. Feel free to copy these and send them home with the children. These offer suggestions for children and parents on how they can keep the lessons fresh and continue learning about God and the Bible throughout the week.

TO SUM UP

Have fun with this curriculum! Enjoy the energy children produce and learn from them as you watch them learn and grow in the things of God.

You may wonder why there isn't anything about praise and worship in this book. I would strongly suggest you include a short time of praise and worship in your class, (no more than ten minutes) but the songs and how you go about it are totally up to you.

The importance of effectively communicating God's Word to children cannot be minimized. This curriculum enables you to fulfill that assignment in creative ways that are fun for teachers and children alike.

If you have questions or comments about anything in this book, you can find my contact information in the back of this book on page 207.

Blessings,
Angela E. Powell

UNIT 1

UNIT THEME: GOD HAS A PLAN FOR YOU AND ME!

In this unit the children will discover God is a God of planning and He has a plan for each one of us. This unit uses a GPS to help explain how God's plans for our lives work.

Lesson 1: Creation of the World

God created the world in a certain order. He planned it out. This lesson will explore the order in which God created the earth and the purpose of all He created. By the end of this lesson, kids will begin to understand God loves them and has a plan for their lives.

Lesson 2: Creation of Man

The creation of man was God's crowning achievement. This lesson explores facts about the human body so the children understand how much detail and planning went into creating our bodies. By the end of the lesson, the kids will better understand that for God to plan our bodies and our earth in such detail, His plans for us must be much greater.

Lesson 3: God's Plan for Everyone

This lesson explains how we find out what God's plan for our life is, through prayer and reading our Bibles. It shows the importance of having a relationship with God and "fueling up" with Him so we can stay on the road He has for us.

Lesson 4: Life's Not Fair But…

This lesson looks at the life of Joseph. Many unfair things happened to him, but he didn't complain or get angry with God. We'll look at how his relationship with God affected his attitude and how sometimes we don't understand how God can use bad things for good, but if we trust Him and keep moving forward, we'll see it eventually.

Lesson 5: God's Plan for Me

God tells us not to worry because He is there for us and has a plan for us. In this lesson, the kids will learn why trusting God is important when it comes to the plans He has for them. This lesson will focus on worry and why God doesn't want us to worry.

Optional Videos For This Unit: http://bit.ly/2j2mv7E

Angela E. Powell

GOD HAS A PLAN FOR YOU AND ME!

SUPPLIES NEEDED		
Copies of take home sheet on page 15	Copy of cards from page 14	GPS
Green and Blue tissue paper	Animal facts video	Toy bugs
Recording of animal sounds	Toy birds	Toy plants
Toy trees	Toy animals	Foam shapes
Prayer Notebooks Glue	Popsicle sticks	Items from nature
Pictures of the sun, moon, and stars	Miscellaneous building materials	

LESSON 1: CREATION OF THE WORLD
WELCOME

As you welcome children to class, have this question written on a white board, piece of paper, or ask the question to each child as you welcome them. Have the children find someone they don't know very well and discuss it.

Ice Breaker Question: If you didn't have to sleep what would you do with the extra time?

GAME
CREATE THE CREATURE

SUPPLIES: Copy of picture cards from page 14, miscellaneous building materials.

- If you have a large group of children, divide them up into groups of no more than four. If your group is small, each child can have their own card to work on.
- Give each team, or child, a card and a box of building materials such as craft sticks or blocks.
- Each group must recreate the image on the card the best they can with the items available.
- Give them seven minutes to complete the task.
- If they are comfortable doing so, have the children present their cards and creations and have them explain how hard or easy it was for them.

LESSON 1: CREATION OF THE WORLD

Play animal sounds and have the children guess which animals are making those sounds. There is a link on the overview page where you can find videos for this unit or you can use your own.

Introduce the lesson by having items from nature such as different shapes, sizes and colors of leaves, sticks or small rocks sitting on a table. Allow the kids to quietly look at and touch the different elements for the first few minutes of the lesson.

God And Me

GOD HAS A PLAN FOR YOU AND ME!

ASK: Who knows what a GPS is?

SAY: It's a device that plans out the best path to get somewhere.

ASK: Did you know God has planned out a path for you as you grow up? Did you know that just like a GPS will tell you to turn right in 500 feet, God will tell you what the next step is in His plan for your life?

SAY: The Bible is also like a GPS. It's Gods map but instead of showing us how to get to a specific place, it shows us the best way to get through life. In the next few weeks we're going to look at different parts of the Bible to find out what God's plan for us is because God has a plan for you and me! God has a plan for everyone!

SAY: The first story we're going to look at is the very first story in the Bible.

ASK: Does anyone know what the first story in the Bible is about?

SAY: It tells us how God created this earth we live in.

ASK: How many of you know how to program an address into a GPS? **(Have the child explain the process)** How did you learn to work a GPS?

SAY: We have to learn how to use a map before we can use it. We learn by watching others and trying it ourselves. So we're going to learn how to use God's map. Pull out your Bible if you have one, or use one of ours.

SAY: The Bible is made up of different books. Each book has a name. The name of the first book in the Bible is Genesis. Every book in the Bible is divided into chapters. Those are the big numbers you'll see in most Bibles. Each chapter is divided into verses. Those are the small numbers. We're going to read from Genesis chapter 1. See if you can find that in your Bibles.

READ THE WORD: Have the kids follow along as the teacher or older kids read the following verses.
Genesis 1:1-5, 6, 8-11, 13-15, 19-20, 23-24, 26, 31

Angela E. Powell

GOD HAS A PLAN FOR YOU AND ME!

HANDS-ON ACTIVITY

SUPPLIES: Blue and Green tissue paper, Sun, moon, and star cut-outs, Foam shapes, Toy animals, Toy plants, Toy bugs, Toy birds.

While the Bible verses are being read, begin building a world with toys, tissue paper, and sun, moon, and star cutouts. You can use small foam shapes to make the sun, moon, and stars stand up. Build the world out of order. Put animals in the sea **(blue tissue paper)** and under the land **(green tissue paper),** and have plants upside down etc.

ASK: Isn't it amazing that God created everything in our world in six days?

SAY: Look! I've created my own version of the world. I included everything in our story: animals, birds, plants, land, water, the sun, the moon, and the stars too! Only, I think there is something wrong with my world.

ASK: What do you guys think? What did I do wrong? **(Put things in the wrong order)** Can you help me fix it?

ASK: (As the kids to put your world in order) If you choose to take a right when your GPS is telling you to take a left what is going to happen?

SAY: It's going to tell you to turn around because you're not going the right way. Just like I didn't follow the right steps when I created my little world.

SAY: God has a plan for you and me and we can see God planned everything, even the order of how He would create the earth!

ASK: How many different animals, insects, and birds do you think we can name together?

SAY: Let's find out! **(Have the kids start naming animals. Write them down or keep track of how many they come up with.)**

ASK: We came up with a lot of animals, but did you know, we didn't even come close to the actual number of animals there are?

God And Me

GOD HAS A PLAN FOR YOU AND ME!

FUN FACTS[1]

There are over 950,000 types of insects, more than 30,000 types of fish, over 8,000 types of reptiles, and more than 9,000 types of birds. On top of that, there are around 10,000 new types of animals found every year!

VIDEO: (Optional) Show a video of animals the kids may have never seen before. There is a link on the overview page where you can find videos for this unit or you can use your own.

ASK: Do any of the animals in the video look like the animals you came up with in our game? Why do you think God made so many different types of bugs, birds, and animals?

SAY: Because God has a plan for you and me! He wants us to enjoy the world He made for us. That is part of His plan for you and me.

ASK: Who has a favorite animal? What is it?

SAY: God made those animals just because He knew you would like them. Isn't that cool? God created the world with a plan in mind. He planned the world to be the perfect place for us to live out the plan He made for each one of us!

MEMORY VERSE

SAY: The Bible, God's GPS for our lives, tells us He has a plan for us. Let's read our memory verse for this unit and see what kind of plans God has for us.

Jeremiah 29:11 - "For I know the plans I have for you," declares the Lord, "plans to prosper you and not to harm you, plans to give you a hope and a future."

SAY: Let's say that together a few times.

ASK: What is this verse telling us?

SAY: God has a plan for you and me! God knows what His plan is for each of us and His plans are good, not bad!

---

[1] https://www.factmonster.com/science/animals/estimated-number-animal-and-plant-species-earth

Angela E. Powell

GOD HAS A PLAN FOR YOU AND ME!

PRAYER CIRCLES - "God With Me" Prayer

As the children learn to pray and hear God's voice, it can be helpful to give them each a notebook so they can keep track of what they hear and are praying for. Keep these notebooks in a safe place in class until you finish this curriculum. Encourage the kids to write down prayer requests they, or their peers have, on the take home sheet so they can be reminded to pray for those things during the week. For more information on this method of prayer, please look in the reference section on page 207.

- Hand each child a notebook they'll be able to use in class for the duration of this curriculum, and a pen or pencil. Tell the kids not to write in their notebooks until they are ready to write what they're hearing from the Lord.
- **Begin with Interactive Gratitude. Have the kids think of two or three things they're grateful for.** At first, they can start with things, but try to encourage them to list what they appreciate about their peers, teachers, parents, and other people they encounter every day.
- **Have the kids write down what they're thankful for in the form of a prayer.** ("God, today I'm thankful for...") Have them be as specific as possible. Instead of just saying they're thankful for their parents, have them come up with a specific reason they're thankful. The more specific they can get, the better.
- **Next, have them write down what they think God would say in response to the things they're grateful for.** This might be difficult at first if the kids don't know God's character very well. You may need to explain that God will always respond to us in love, and any judgmental, hurtful, or negative thoughts that come to their minds is not from God.
- **After the Interactive Gratitude is complete, have the kids take several deep breaths.** This will help calm their minds and bodies so they can better participate in the next portion.
- **Once everyone appears calm and relaxed, have them write down some things they want to pray about.** Have them write these things down as though God were sitting next to them having a conversation with them. ("God, the bully at school is really bothering me.") To begin, it might be best to keep things simple. Have them pray for things on their radar: bullies at school, a subject in school they're struggling with, their parent's jobs, their siblings. At this point, we don't want them to go too deep until they really start understanding how to hear God's voice.
- If they have trouble coming up with subjects, give them some ideas such as praying they sleep well at night, or get up on time, or if they're willing they can pray for God to give them a desire to get to know Him. As long as the prayer is true for them they can pray about it. We don't want them to pray just to go through the motions.
- **Once they have one or two items, have them write as though God were responding to them. Begin with how God sees them.** For example "I see you sitting in your classroom wondering what to pray about. I see how concerned you are about this issue. I see how worried you are about this."

GOD HAS A PLAN FOR YOU AND ME!

- **Once they've written a sentence or two on that, move to "I hear you".** For example, "I hear you crying at night about this issue. I hear you telling me you want me to fix this. I hear you telling your parents how worried you are about the bully at school."
- **Next, have them write a couple of sentences that start with "I'm glad to be with you."** For example, "I'm glad to be with you right now as you tell me about this issue. I'm glad to be with you when you're crying in your bed at night. I'm glad to be with you even when you're struggling with negative emotions."
- There is more to this prayer method, but we will add on in other lessons. For now, this is a good introduction.
- **Finally, if anyone wants to share what God said to them, allow them some time for this.** This is an important step, and if you are able to spend time during the week before class practicing this method, it will help the kids be more comfortable with sharing if you are able to share from your own notebook.

Angela E. Powell

GOD HAS A PLAN FOR YOU AND ME!

GOD HAS A PLAN FOR YOU AND ME AT HOME!

LESSON SUMMARY: Today we learned God created the earth in a certain order and He is a God who has a plan for everything. He planned out the order of how the earth should be made because He has a plan for each one of us in this earth. We also learned that just like a GPS will tell us to turn right in 500 feet, God will tell us the next step He wants us to take in the plan He has for us.

MEMORY VERSE: Jeremiah 29:11 - "For I know the plans I have for you," declares the Lord, "plans to prosper you and not to harm you, plans to give you a hope and a future."

IN THE CAR
- Look for animals or birds as you're driving around town. Talk about the different types you see.
- Find out if anyone in your family knows any fun facts about the animals or birds you see.
- Thank God for all the animals or birds you see.
- Have a contest to see who can spot the most animals or birds.

AT MEALTIMES
- Talk about what everyone has planned for the day or week ahead.
- Plan dinner for the following evening, assign everyone a task and make dinner together.
- Before anyone puts food on their plate, have everyone come up with a plan on how to pass the food around the table. Make it fun! Have everyone use hand motions instead of words to indicate what they want, or use chopsticks to serve the food instead of spoons.

AT BEDTIME
- Pray and ask God to show you His plan for your life.
- Talk to your parents about how God speaks to them.
- Practice your memory verse as you get ready for bed.

PRAYER REQUESTS:

© 2019 Angela E. Powell

Angela E. Powell

GOD HAS A PLAN FOR YOU AND ME!

SUPPLIES NEEDED

Copies of take home sheet on page 20
1-4 ¼ Measuring cups
Dandelion facts video
Prayer Notebooks

Two buckets
Timer
Dandelions

One gallon jug of water
GPS
Human body facts video

LESSON 2: CREATION OF MAN

WELCOME

As you welcome children to class, have this question written on a white board, piece of paper, or ask the question to each child as you welcome them. Have the children find someone they don't know very well and discuss it.

Ice Breaker Question: What would your perfect room look like?

GAME
(HEART)BEAT THE CLOCK [2]

SUPPLIES: 2 buckets, 1 gallon jug of water, 1/4 Measuring cups, Timer

BEFORE CLASS: If you have a large group, you'll need four, 1/4 measuring cups. If your group is small, you can get away with one. These can usually be found at used goods stores or yard sales for cheap. You can also experiment with different sized plastic cups and use cups that equal about 1/4 cup.

SAY: In one day **(24 hours)** the heart pumps about 1,900 gallons of blood. So every single minute your heart pumps a little over one gallon of blood, or about ¼ of a cup every second! **(Hold up the gallon jug to show how much blood the heart pumps in a minute, then hold up the measuring cup to show the amount pumped every second.)**

- Divide kids into teams of no more than four.
- Give each group one minute to transfer one gallon of water from one bucket to another using the measuring cups.
- If you have a really small group, time each child by themselves.

---

[2] "Human Body Activities: The Heart." Used with permission. *Primary Theme Park*. Stephanie Trapp, 18 Oct. 2016. Web. <www.primarythemepark.com>.

God And Me

GOD HAS A PLAN FOR YOU AND ME!

LESSON 2: CREATION OF MAN

SAY: Last week we talked about how a GPS is a map that gives us directions on how to get somewhere. We compared a GPS to God's plan for our lives because just like a GPS can plan a path for us to take, God has a plan for how He wants us to live our lives.

ASK: What else can a GPS do?

SAY: It can show us where gas stations are so we can stop for fuel when we're getting low. It can show us where we can stop for food if we get hungry. Some of them will tell you if the traffic is bad or if there is construction. A GPS does more than one thing. God made everything so it could be used in a lot of ways.

ASK: Who knows what a dandelion is? Did you know God made dandelions for a reason?

SAY: He had a plan for dandelions and it wasn't just so we could cut it down with a lawnmower or weed wacker. Most people consider dandelions to be nothing but a weed, but God planned them to be so much more than that.

SHOW VIDEO AND/OR GIVE THE FOLLOWING FACTS [3]
NOTE: There is a link on the overview page where you can find videos for this unit or you can use your own.
- At one time, Dandelions were used to make yellow dye for fabrics
- Dandelions are edible and are a rich source of vitamins A, C, and K. They also contain a high level of Iron, Calcium, and Potassium.
- The roots of Dandelions can be used to make a coffee substitute.
- Dandelion can be used to treat infections and liver disorders.
- The milky liquid made in the stems of a dandelion contains latex, a substance similar to rubber. This type of latex could be used to replace the rubber found in the tires on our cars.

ASK: Did you know dandelions could be used for so many things?

SAY: God planned for dandelions to be all of those things and more!

ASK: Did you know God made our bodies to do a lot of different things too?

---

[3] Dandelion Facts. (n.d.). Retrieved November 30, 2017, from http://www.softschools.com/facts/plants/dandelion_facts/597/

GOD HAS A PLAN FOR YOU AND ME!

SAY: He made our bodies so they could heal after getting a cut, scratch, or broken bone. He made them strong so we can run, jump, and play. He gave us our five senses so we could enjoy the world He created for us and learn to stay away from things that could hurt us, like fire!

ASK: How boring would it be if you couldn't taste or smell any of the food you ate?

SAY: Let's find out some cool things about our bodies.

WATCH VIDEO AND/OR GIVE THE FOLLOWING FACTS.[4]
NOTE: There is a link on the overview page where you can find videos for this unit or you can use your own.
- Your mouth makes 1.75 pints **(1 liter)** of saliva every day!
- Human teeth are just as strong as shark teeth!
- Your hands, wrists and fingers are made up of 54 bones!
- Hair is so strong some people think the hair on one person's head could hold the weight of two elephants. That theory has never been tested though.

SAY: God has a plan for you and me. He made our bodies strong to do what He planned for us. But how did He make our bodies? Let's open our Bibles, God's map for our lives, and find out. We'll read from the book of Genesis, chapter 2, verses 7-9 and 18-22. Remember, big numbers are chapters, little numbers are verses.

READ THE WORD: Have the kids follow along as the teacher or older kids read the following verses. **Genesis 2:7-9, 18-22.**

SAY: The Bible doesn't give us a lot of detail about how He designed our bodies, but He put so much detail and planned for our bodies to do so many things that even though scientists and doctors have been studying the human body for thousands of years, they are still finding new things all the time.

SAY: God has a plan for you and me, and just like a GPS can show us more than how to get somewhere, God created us to be able to do a lot of different things. All of these things can help us live out God's plan for our lives. For example, you aren't just kids. You're students, sports players, music lovers, musicians, game players, friends, brothers or sisters, and sons or daughters.

---

[4] https://www.natgeokids.com/uk/discover/science/general-science/15-facts-about-the-human-body/

GOD HAS A PLAN FOR YOU AND ME!

SAY: You are all of these things and each one looks a little bit different. When you're being a friend you're learning to be kind, to share, and to have relationships with people who aren't in your family. God has a plan for all of your friendships. He also has a plan for you as a son or daughter, and a plan for you as a student. All of these things are leading you, like a GPS, to God's future plans for your life.

MEMORY VERSE

ASK: Who can remember which book, chapter and verse our memory verse is from?

Jeremiah 29:11 - "For I know the plans I have for you," declares the Lord, "plans to prosper you and not to harm you, plans to give you a hope and a future."

SAY: Last week we talked about how this verse tells us God's plans for us are good, not bad. But He also tells us what that means for our future.

ASK: What does this verse say about God's plans for our future? What does it mean if you're hopeful about your future?

PRAYER CIRCLES - Groups

As the children learn to pray and hear God's voice, it can be helpful to give them each a notebook so they can keep track of what they hear and are praying for. Keep these notebooks in a safe place in class until you finish this curriculum. Encourage the kids to write down prayer requests they, or their peers have, on the take home sheet so they can be reminded to pray for those things during the week.

- Have kids get into groups of three or four with at least one older child or leader in each group who can keep the kids on task.
- Have the kids share their prayer requests with the others in their group.
- Encourage each child to pray for one of the prayer requests presented.
- If no one has any prayer requests or there aren't enough for everyone to pray about, give them suggestions such as praying for a good, safe week for everyone in the church or God would bring in more kids.
- If some groups finish before others, encourage the children to write down the prayer requests they heard in their group and/or spend time trying to hear God's voice.

Angela E. Powell

GOD HAS A PLAN FOR YOU AND ME AT HOME!

LESSON SUMMARY: Today we looked at how God made our bodies and learned some interesting facts about them. We also learned about dandelions and how God planned for them to be much more than a weed. In the same way, a GPS can do more than show us how to get from point A to point B, and likewise, we were created for more than one purpose.

MEMORY VERSE: Jeremiah 29:11 - "For I know the plans I have for you," declares the Lord, "plans to prosper you and not to harm you, plans to give you a hope and a future."

IN THE CAR
- What does your car smell like?
- Play the alphabet game. Find things outside the car that begin with each letter of the alphabet. Or, play a variation of the game by thinking of a smell that begins with each letter. For example: A smells like apple juice. B smells like bad breath.
- If you have a GPS in your car or on your phone, have it give you directions home. As you drive, pay attention to what else it shows you on the map as you drive.

AT MEALTIMES
- Talk about the sounds you hear during dinner.
- Plan to eat dinner somewhere else, at a restaurant, or even in a different room in your house, or outside in the backyard. Discuss the different sounds in the different locations.
- Talk about how the food tastes and what it would be like if we couldn't taste our food.
- Thank God for our five senses when you pray over the meal.

AT BEDTIME
- Pray and ask God to show you His plan for your life.
- Practice your memory verse as you get ready for bed.
- Pay attention to what things feel like as you get ready for bed. The toothbrush against your teeth, your pj's, your sheets and blankets, the floor on your bare feet. Thank God for your five senses.

PRAYER REQUESTS:

God And Me

GOD HAS A PLAN FOR YOU AND ME!

SUPPLIES NEEDED

Copies of take home sheet on page 28	Small boxes	Marbles
Clue cards on pages 26-27	GPS	Candy
How to pray videos	Prayer Notebooks	

LESSON 3: GOD'S PLAN FOR EVERYONE

WELCOME

As you welcome children to class, have this question written on a white board, piece of paper, or ask the question to each child as you welcome them. Have the children find someone they don't know very well and discuss it.

Ice Breaker Question: What fictional place would you most like to go?

GAME

LIVE BY EXAMPLE

SUPPLIES: Small boxes, Marbles

- Have enough boxes for each child to have one.
- Put three marbles in the bottom of two boxes and give each child a box. Only two kids will have a box with marbles in it.
- If a child gets a box with marbles in it, they have to try and keep it a secret that they have the marbles.
- Give instructions to the kids such as "Stand up, sit down, turn around".
- After every few instructions, ask if anyone wants to guess who has the marbles.
- Make the instructions more difficult as you go along. "Jump twice, stand on one foot, etc."
- Discuss how the kids acted when they had marbles in their boxes. What gave them away?

LESSON 3: GOD'S PLAN FOR EVERYONE

SAY: We've been talking about how a GPS is a map that gives us directions on how to get somewhere. We know a GPS can get us to where we want to go, and we also talked about how it can show us things like gas stations and places to get food along the way. We compared a GPS to God's plan for our lives because just like a GPS can plan a path for us to take, God has a plan for how He wants us to live our lives. And just like a GPS can do more than one thing, everything God created can do more than one thing, especially our bodies.

Angela E. Powell

GOD HAS A PLAN FOR YOU AND ME!

SAY: God has a plan for you and me and that big plan for your life is full of smaller plans.

ASK: Did you know you can program more than one stop into a GPS?

SAY: Let's say you wanted to go to your grandma's house, but she lives in another state. You know you're going to need to stop for food and get fuel for your car. You can tell your GPS to go to grandma's house, but you can also plan stops along the way at gas stations and stores. The GPS will take you to all of those places in one trip.

SAY: God has a plan for you and me. Sometimes we have to learn some things before we can find out what God wants us to do next. The Bible, God's map for our lives, tells us there are some things we all need to do in order to find out the rest of God's plan for our lives. We're going to play a game to help you understand what I'm talking about.

GAME: SCAVENGER HUNT FOR CLUES
You can use the clue cards on pages 26-27 or make up your own. Just be sure the kids have to figure out a problem or puzzle before they are able to read the clues. If you have a lot of kids, you can print out multiple clue cards and have each team race to find them all.

SAY: This game is called Scavenger Hunt For Clues, and I have the first clue here. It will tell you where to look for the second clue. **(Read clue #1)**

SAY: (When the game is over) Each clue led to the next clue, but even after you found each clue you had to figure some things out before you could figure out the next step. Life is like that. Sometimes we have to figure out some things before we can grow in certain areas.

ASK: Where can we find clues about God's plan for our lives?

SAY: The Bible! God has a plan for you and me and we're going to find out what part of that plan is in the book of First Timothy, chapter 2, verses 1-5.

ASK: Remember how we talked about the Bible being a bunch of different books with different names?

SAY: There are two books called Timothy, so we call them First and Second Timothy. They are near the back of your Bible. You can look at the Table of Contents in the front of your Bible to see what page First Timothy starts on.

God And Me

GOD HAS A PLAN FOR YOU AND ME!

READ THE WORD: Have the kids follow along as the teacher or older kids read the following verses.
1 Timothy 2:1-5

SAY: God tells us part of His plan for our lives is to pray for people.

ASK: What kind of people? **(All people!)** Why does God want us to pray?

SAY: The number one reason is to talk to Him so we can have a relationship with Him. Our Bibles are like God's map for our lives.

ASK: Are we going to know what we're supposed to do if we don't read the map?

SAY: No!

ASK: But what if we read the map and don't understand it?

SAY: We can pray and ask God, the creator of the map, to help us understand it.

ASK: How do we pray?

WATCH VIDEO(S) ABOUT PRAYER
There is a link on the overview page where you can find videos for this unit or you can use your own.

SAY: God has a plan for you and me and just like we have to stop and put gas in our cars so our cars can keep going down the road, we have to fill our hearts and minds up. We do that through prayer and reading our Bibles.

ASK: Do you think a GPS will still tell you how to get to your grandma's house even though your car has run out of gas and is sitting on the side of the road?

SAY: Yes, the directions are still there, but you're stuck until you can put more gas in your car. God's plan for us is to fill ourselves up with His Bible and have a relationship with Him. It's easier to get where you're going if you keep your car filled up with gas than if you're always letting the gas run out before you fill the tank.

GOD HAS A PLAN FOR YOU AND ME!

SAY: We can run out of energy while we're on our journey of God's plan for our lives. God wants us to fill up every day by talking to Him and reading our Bibles, which is one reason we have memory verses for you to learn.

MEMORY VERSE

SAY: Let's say our memory verse a few times.

Jeremiah 29:11 - "For I know the plans I have for you," declares the Lord, "plans to prosper you and not to harm you, plans to give you a hope and a future."

SAY: It might seem like prayer and reading the Bible are boring things to do. If that's the case, pray and ask God to show you why His Bible is so interesting. Our memory verse tells us all of God's plans for us are good, and not meant to harm us. So if prayer and reading our Bibles is part of that plan, then it must be good for us.

PRAYER CIRCLES - "God With Me" Prayer

As the children learn to pray and hear God's voice, it can be helpful to give them each a notebook so they can keep track of what they hear and are praying for. Keep these notebooks in a safe place in class until you finish this curriculum. Encourage the kids to write down prayer requests they, or their peers have, on the take home sheet so they can be reminded to pray for those things during the week. For more information on this method of prayer, please look in the reference section on page 207.

- Hand each child a notebook they'll be able to use in class for the duration of this curriculum, and a pen or pencil. Tell the kids not to write in their notebooks until they are ready to write what they're hearing from the Lord.
- **Begin with Interactive Gratitude. Have the kids think of two or three things they're grateful for.** At first, they can start with things, but try to encourage them to think about what they appreciate about their peers, teachers, parents, and other people they encounter every day.
- **Have the kids write down what they're thankful for in the form of a prayer.** ("God, today I'm thankful for...") Have them be as specific as possible. Instead of just saying they're thankful for their parents, have them come up with a specific reason they're thankful. The more specific they can get, the better.
- **Next, have them write down what they think God would say in response to the things they're grateful for.** This might be difficult at first if the kids don't know God's character very well. You may need to explain that God will always respond to us in love, and any judgmental, hurtful, or negative thoughts that come to their minds is not from God.
- **After the Interactive Gratitude is complete, have the kids take several deep breaths.** This will help calm their minds and bodies so they can better participate in the next portion.

GOD HAS A PLAN FOR YOU AND ME!

- **Once everyone appears calm and relaxed, have them write down some things they want to pray about.** Have them write these things down as though God were sitting next to them having a conversation with them. ("God, the bully at school is really bothering me.") To begin, it might be best to keep things simple. Have them pray for things on their radar: bullies at school, a subject in school they're struggling with, their parent's jobs, their siblings. At this point, we don't want them to go too deep until they really start understanding how to hear God's voice.
- If they have trouble coming up with subjects, give them some ideas such as praying they sleep well at night, or get up on time, or if they're willing they can pray for God to give them a desire to get to know Him. As long as the prayer is true for them they can pray about it. We don't want them to pray just to go through the motions.
- **Once they have one or two items, have them write as though God were responding to them. Begin with how God sees them.** For example, "I see you sitting in your classroom wondering what to pray about. I see how concerned you are about this issue. I see how worried you are about this."
- **Once they've written a sentence or two on that, move to "I hear you".** For example, "I hear you crying at night about this issue. I hear you telling Me you want Me to fix this. I hear you telling your parents how worried you are about the bully at school."
- **Next, have them write a couple sentences that start with "I understand how hard this is for you."** For example, "I understand how hard it is for you to go to school every day knowing there is a bully there, waiting." There may be some things the kids pray about that this wouldn't apply to. If that is the case, they can skip this step.
- **Next, have them write a couple of sentences that start with "I'm glad to be with you."** For example, "I'm glad to be with you right now as you tell me about this issue. I'm glad to be with you when you're crying in your bed at night. I'm glad to be with you even when you're struggling with negative emotions."
- **The last writing prompt to give them is, "I can do something about what you're going through."** This one might be harder if the kids don't understand God's character. In this case, God might respond by giving us a Bible verse reminding us of His goodness, His love, His faithfulness, etc. or He might remind us of a time in our past when we got through another difficult situation. Here is an example of what He might say, "I will help you continue to see more clearly who I am and what I've been doing in your life. I am protecting you. When you're feeling scared, remember I'm with you." Remind the kids that God will only say things that are loving, kind, and compassionate.
- **Finally, if anyone wants to share what God said to them, allow them some time for this.** This is an important step, and if you are able to spend time during the week before class practicing this method, it will help the kids be more comfortable with sharing if you are able to share from your own notebook.

GOD HAS A PLAN FOR YOU AND ME!

Clue # 1

We have a stack of extras

For anyone who's new.

If you were in a rush today, there's one

in there for you!

TIPS: Keep clue #1 with you. Cut clue #2 into 9 pieces and put inside an envelope so they have to put a puzzle together. Fold clue #3 into an origami envelope. Clue #4 is a riddle for them to solve. Cut clue #5 into 9 pieces to make another puzzle.

ANSWERS Clue #1 – Look for the next clue in a stack of extra Bibles. **Clue #2** – Look for the next clue under a table. **Clue #3** – Behind something that begins with the letter "C", taped to a box of Crayons, Cubby, etc. **Clue #4** – Look for the last clue under their chairs. **Clue #5** – The last clue leads to a treat from you!

Clue #2

I HAVE FOUR LEGS BUT DON'T HAVE ARMS.

I SERVE FOOD THAT COMES FROM FARMS.

I HAVE FOUR LEGS BUT CANNOT RUN.

Clue #3

HINT: The words themselves are not important when it Comes to finding Clue #4.

"Clues in Cubes are Crucial to Completing your Case."

© 2019 Angela E. Powell

GOD HAS A PLAN FOR YOU AND ME!

Clue #4

If you have a clock and remove the lock, then add a head of hair, you'll find me under there.

Clue #5

Learning, Teaching, Smiling Face I see you once a week.

Games, Fun, Bible Stories, Memory Verses, and Prayer.

I have a treat for you. Can you guess who I am?

Don't Let On Please! Come Quietly Then take your seat!

GOD HAS A PLAN FOR YOU AND ME AT HOME!

LESSON SUMMARY: Today we talked about how a GPS can get us to more than one place in one trip. We can program a GPS to take us to the gas station, a fast food restaurant, and grandma's house. In the same way, God's big plan for our life includes a lot of smaller steps and plans along the way.

MEMORY VERSE: Jeremiah 29:11 - "For I know the plans I have for you," declares the Lord, "plans to prosper you and not to harm you, plans to give you a hope and a future."

IN THE CAR
- Pray for a safe trip to wherever you're going.
- When you're stopped at a light, pay attention to the cars next to you. Pray for those people to have a safe trip to where they're going.
- Try programming multiple stops into your GPS when you're out running errands with the kids and discuss how God has a plan for their lives.

AT MEALTIMES
- Pray for the people who made your meal.
- Ask your family for ideas of things and people to pray about.
- Ask your family why prayer is important to them.

AT BEDTIME
- Pray and ask God to show you His plan for your life.
- Practice your memory verse as you get ready for bed.
- Think about your day. Thank God for the good things that happened.
- Pray for your family.

PRAYER REQUESTS:

God And Me

GOD HAS A PLAN FOR YOU AND ME!

SUPPLIES NEEDED		
Copies of take home sheet on page 35	GPS	Chairs
Copies of maze on page 34	Music	Joseph's journey video
Prayer Notebooks		

LESSON 4: LIFE'S NOT FAIR BUT...
WELCOME

As you welcome children to class, have this question written on a white board, piece of paper, or ask the question to each child as you welcome them. Have the children find someone they don't know very well and discuss it.

Ice Breaker Question: What skill would you like to master?

GAME
MUSICAL CHAIRS WITH A TWIST

SUPPLIES: Chairs, Music

- Play a game of musical chairs, but introduce special "unfair" rules before each round.
- These special rules could include things like, "Everyone with blonde hair gets to remain seated". Or "If you're wearing the same color shirt as the teacher you can't lose this round." Or "If you're wearing jewelry you have to hop instead of run".
- Do this several times so everyone has a chance to experience an unfair rule in a positive and negative way.
- Explain that our lesson today is about someone who had a lot of unfair things happen to him.

LESSON 4: LIFE'S NOT FAIR BUT...

SAY: We've been talking about how a GPS is like God's plan for our lives.

ASK: What kinds of things can a GPS do and how can they remind us of God's plan for our lives?

SAY: A GPS will give us directions to a place. Praying and reading the Bible can help us navigate God's plan for our lives. A GPS can do more than get us to one place. It can show us where we can stop and fill up with food and fuel, and it can get us to more than one place in a single trip. Inside God's big plan for our lives are a lot of little plans and sometimes we have to figure a few things out before we can move to the next step.

Angela E. Powell

GOD HAS A PLAN FOR YOU AND ME!

ASK: Why does a GPS give us one direction at a time?

SAY: When you're driving you have to pay attention to a lot of different things. The cars around you, road signs, traffic lights, and even the weather. So if the GPS gave us more than one direction at a time we might get confused or lost.

SAY: Last week we talked about how God wants us to fill up on prayer and reading the Bible.

ASK: Does anyone remember what happens if we don't fill up with prayer and the Bible?

SAY: We run out of energy. We're like a car that ran out of gas. God's plan is still there, but we have to fill ourselves up again before we can continue on our journey.

ASK: Why do we lose energy?

SAY: Sometimes life isn't very fun. We get sick or injured. Friends move away or we get into fights with our friends and they don't want to be friends with us anymore. Sometimes life doesn't seem fair, just like with the game we played today. All those things can cause us to lose energy. So we need to fill up with God's goodness, kindness, and love so we can keep going.

ASK: Have you ever gone on a trip and the GPS stopped working or wasn't working the way it should?

SAY: It's really frustrating, especially if you don't know where you're going. Sometimes you put in an address and the directions take you somewhere you didn't want to go, or sometimes you might run into construction and the whole road is blocked off so you have to ask the GPS for another way, or maybe the battery isn't charged and the GPS won't turn on, or turns off while you're driving.

OPTIONAL: Show GPS Fail video.
There is a link on the overview page where you can find videos for this unit or you can use your own.

ASK: Did you know, even when life is frustrating or doesn't seem fair, God still has a plan for you and me?

SAY: We're going to read **(or watch)** a story from the Bible, God's map for our lives, about a man who had a lot of unfair things happen to him. This story is in the book of Genesis, the first book of the Bible. We're going to look at a couple of chapters, but we're going to start in chapter 37.

God And Me

GOD HAS A PLAN FOR YOU AND ME!

READ THE WORD: Have the kids follow along as the teacher or older kids read the following verses. Since this is a long passage of scripture you can use videos that tell the story of Joseph. **Genesis 37:2-25, 39:1-6, 20-23, 41:14-16, 37-40. Stop reading/watching after each event in Joseph's life and discuss what is happening. There is a link where you can find videos on the unit overview page for this unit or you can use your own.**

ASK: (After Joseph is sold as a servant) Was it fair that Joseph's brothers sold him as a slave? Do you think this was part of God's plan for Joseph?

SAY: Let's keep reading/watching and find out.

ASK: (After Joseph is put in prison) Do you think it was fair that Potiphar's wife told lies about Joseph? Do you think this was part of God's plan for Joseph?

SAY: Let's keep reading/watching to find out.

ASK: (After Pharaoh's servant forgets about Joseph) Do you think it was fair that the servant of Pharaoh forgot about Joseph and he had to stay in prison? Do you think THIS was part of God's plan for Joseph?

SAY: Let's keep reading/watching to find out.

ASK: (When the video is over) Do you think it was God's plan for Joseph to save his family and hundreds of other people from the famine?

SAY: Yes!

ASK: Remember the dreams Joseph had and told his brothers about?

SAY: That was God's way of saying "Hey Joseph, I have a plan for you and one day you're going to be a powerful person and people are going to bow down to you, including your family!" That was a promise!

Angela E. Powell

GOD HAS A PLAN FOR YOU AND ME!

HANDS-ON ACTIVITY (Optional)

SUPPLIES: Joseph's maze printout from page 34

- If the kids start getting restless at this point, you can take a break here and have them complete Joseph's Maze.
- It's a 3-in-1 maze you can use to explain how Joseph could have given up at each stop along his journey, but he didn't.
- TIP: Have the kids use a different colored pencil for each path.

SAY: When Joseph was sold as a servant Joseph could have gotten angry with God. He could have said, "God, you promised I would be a powerful person, but now I'm a servant. People don't bow down to servants, this isn't fair!"

SAY: He could have gotten angry again when Potiphar's wife lied about him and he went to jail, or when Pharaoh's servant forgot about him. Instead, he reminded himself of God's promise because he prayed and had a relationship with God and knew God's plan was meant for good and not for harm.

ASK: Isn't that what our memory verse says? Did you know Joseph knew that even though the man who wrote that verse, Jeremiah, wasn't even alive yet?

SAY: When God tells us something, you can trust Him because He never changes and His plans are always good. Joseph had a lot of reasons to be angry, but instead He chose to trust that all of those unfair things were part of God's plan. He even says in Genesis chapter 47 verse 5, "Don't be distressed and do not be angry with yourselves for selling me here, because it was to save lives that God sent me ahead of you."

SAY: It's like when we tell our GPS to take us to the toy store, but it takes us to a gas station instead. We can get angry with the GPS, or we can check out gas tank, fill it with gas, get a snack and figure out how we're going to get to the toy store from there.

SAY: Sometimes God lets us go through traffic jams and construction zones to teach us something.

ASK: What did Joseph learn while he worked for Potiphar?

GOD HAS A PLAN FOR YOU AND ME!

SAY: He learned how to manage Potiphar's properties. This would help him later when he had to manage all the extra food to make sure thousands of people had enough food to eat. God has a plan for you and me and sometimes we have to learn some lessons that aren't fun to learn and don't seem fair, but God promises it's all for our good. Let's review our memory verse now.

MEMORY VERSE

SAY: Let's say our memory verse a few times.

Jeremiah 29:11 - "For I know the plans I have for you," declares the Lord, "plans to prosper you and not to harm you, plans to give you a hope and a future."

SAY: Life isn't always fair, but God can use those unfair things to teach us what we need to know in order to get to the next step of His plan for our lives. I hope when life is frustrating or isn't fair, that you'll remember this verse and feel hope.

PRAYER CIRCLES - Groups

As the children are learning to pray and hear God's voice, it can be helpful to give them each a notebook where they can write down what they're hearing and keep track of what they've been praying for. Keep these notebooks in class until you finish this curriculum. Encourage the kids to write down prayer requests they, or their peers have on the take home sheet so they can be reminded to pray for those things during the week.

- Have kids get into groups of three or four with at least one older child or leader in each group.
- Have the kids share their prayer requests with the others in their group.
- Encourage each child to pray for one of the prayer requests presented.
- If no one has prayer requests or there aren't enough for everyone to pray about, give them suggestions such as, praying for a good, safe week for everyone or God would bring in more kids.
- If some groups finish before others, encourage the children to write down the prayer requests they heard in their group and/or spend time trying to hear God's voice.

GOD HAS A PLAN FOR YOU AND ME!

God And Me

GOD HAS A PLAN FOR YOU AND ME AT HOME!

LESSON SUMMARY: Today we looked at why a GPS only gives us one direction at a time instead of all of them at once. We talked about how hard, confusing and overwhelming it would be to remember them all as we're driving. God is the same way. He only gives us one step at a time when He's showing us what His plan for our lives is so we don't get confused or overwhelmed. We also looked at how a GPS isn't perfect and it doesn't always get us where we want to go, then we looked at the life of Joseph and how he had a lot of unfair things happen to him, but God had a plan for Joseph and used those unfair things to get Joseph where God wanted him. We also have unfair things happen to us, but we can trust God to use those things in His plan for us.

MEMORY VERSE: Jeremiah 29:11 - "For I know the plans I have for you," declares the Lord, "plans to prosper you and not to harm you, plans to give you a hope and a future."

IN THE CAR
- Whenever there is a traffic jam, talk about why God might have you there. Maybe He has angels stopping the traffic to prevent an accident from happening.
- Talk about the unfair things that happened during the day and what you can learn from those situations.
- Have each person think of one unfair thing that's happened to them recently and come up with something positive about it. Either a lesson learned through the situation, a way we can change our thinking about someone or something, such as considering that a bully has a lot of fear and that's why they act the way they do, or imagine ways God could use that situation for good.

AT MEALTIMES
- Ask your parents if they pray whenever something upsets them.
- Ask your parents about times when God has used hard times for their good.
- Talk about times when God has blessed each of you.

AT BEDTIME
- Pray and ask God to show you His plan for your life.
- Practice your memory verse as you get ready for bed.
- Think about your day. Talk to God about things that upset you.

PRAYER REQUESTS:

Angela E. Powell

GOD HAS A PLAN FOR YOU AND ME!

SUPPLIES NEEDED
- Copies of take home sheet on page 42
- GPS
- Tables
- Bird catching a worm video
- Plastic cups
- Blind folds
- Boxes
- Miscellaneous items from around the room.
- Ping-pong balls
- Chairs
- Prayer Notebooks

LESSON 5: GOD'S PLAN FOR ME

WELCOME

As you welcome children to class, have this question written on a white board, piece of paper, or ask the question to each child as you welcome them. Have the children find someone they don't know very well and discuss it.

Ice Breaker Question: What would be the most amazing adventure to go on?

GAME

PING PONG BALL DROP

SUPPLIES: Plastic cups, Ping-pong balls, Chairs

- If you have a lot of kids, you might want to split them into teams and race against each other.
- Have one child stand on a chair.
- Put the plastic cup on the floor in front of them.
- The object is to get three ping-pong balls into the cup without them bouncing out, or knocking the cup over.
- If you're doing this in teams or groups, the kids can switch as soon as they get one ball to stay in the cup. The first team to have each person in their team get a ball into the cup wins.

LESSON 5: GOD'S PLAN FOR ME

SAY: We've been talking about how a GPS is like God's plan for our lives.

ASK: What kinds of things can a GPS do and how can they remind us of God's plan for our lives?

SAY: God has a plan for you and me. We learned a GPS can plan a path for us to take, and God has a path for us to take. We learned a GPS can do more than one thing, and everything God created was made for more than one reason.

God And Me

GOD HAS A PLAN FOR YOU AND ME!

SAY: Then we talked about how part of God's plan for our lives is to pray and read our Bibles and if we don't stop and fill our cars up with fuel, they'll eventually run out and we'll be stuck on the side of the road until someone can help us. Last week we looked at the story of Joseph in the Bible. He went through a lot of unfair things, but God used those things for good because God's plans are always good.

ASK: When you use a GPS to get somewhere, do you worry about getting lost or making the wrong turn?

SAY: Not really. God has a plan for you and me and He wants to guide us through that plan the same way a GPS guides us to a destination. Life can be full of ups and downs and lots of choices to make every day. When we don't know which choice to make it can be scary, frustrating, and it can make us worry.

SAY: God doesn't want us to worry. He wants us to trust Him to take care of us. Let's play a game to show what that might look like.

HANDS-ON ACTIVITY

SUPPLIES: Blindfolds, Items for an obstacle course

- Divide kids into teams of two and blindfold one of the children in each team.
- Once one child from each team is blindfolded, create an obstacle course using chairs, tables, boxes, or other easily accessible classroom furniture.
- Explain the course to the children who are not blindfolded and show them the way through it.
- Have the children who are not blindfolded lead the blindfolded person through the course by guiding them by the arm and telling them what to do.
- When all the blindfolded children have gone through, have the other child in the team wear the blindfold. Change the course a little bit.
- Repeat so all the kids have a chance to go through the course blindfolded.

ASK: (When the game is over) Were any of you worried about tripping or running into something?

SAY: If you had a good guide you didn't need to worry. If you had a guide who didn't give very good instructions than you might have worried a little bit.

ASK: How worried would you have been if you'd had no guide at all?

SAY: Earlier I said the Bible tells us not to worry. Let's look at those verses now. We're going to read from the book of Matthew. This is the first book in the New Testament. When you find Matthew, turn to chapter 6. We're going to look at verses 25-34.

Angela E. Powell

GOD HAS A PLAN FOR YOU AND ME!

READ THE WORD: Have the kids follow along as the teacher or older kids read the following verses. **Matthew 6:25-34**

SAY: God has a plan for you and me and He wants us to trust Him no matter what!

ASK: Remember how we talked about Joseph last week?

SAY: He could have worried that his brothers had messed up God's plan for his life, but He chose to trust God more than his brothers.

ASK: What are two things we've talked about God wanting us all to do?

SAY: Read our Bibles, our map from God to get through life, and pray.

ASK: Remember when we talked about prayer being like a gas station stop on our GPS? How often should we fill up?

SAY: Every day!

ASK: What happens if we don't pray or read our Bibles for a long time?

SAY: We run out of energy to keep going down the path God wants us to go down, just like our car runs out of gas if we don't stop to fill it up.

ASK: If we don't pray regularly how will we be able to hear God when He tells us we need to turn right in one mile? Or will school, friends, family, and other life issues drown out the noise?

SAY: If you have the radio up too loud in your car, you won't be able to hear the GPS when it tells you to turn right. You might be able to see it, just like reading your Bible can show you where to go if you read it every day, but if your favorite song comes on and you're jamming to it instead of keeping your eye on the GPS, you're going to miss your turn.

ASK: How can we keep our focus on God so we don't worry about all the stuff happening around us?

SAY: Pray, read the Bible, talk to others about what we're reading in the Bible.

ASK: What did God say about the birds in our Bible reading today? Does anyone remember?

God And Me

GOD HAS A PLAN FOR YOU AND ME!

SAY: God told us to look at the birds if we're feeling worried about something. He said, "Look, they don't plant food or gather food to last them all winter long, but I, **(God)**, feed them." Then He said we're more valuable to Him than the birds.

ASK: If we're more valuable to God than the birds are, but He makes sure the birds get the food they need, don't you think God will take care of your needs too?

SAY: (Optional) lets watch a video to see how a robin catches a worm.

WATCH VIDEO(S)
There is a link on the overview page where you can find videos for this unit or you can use your own.

SAY: A GPS can get you where you want to go and God can get you where He wants you to go. So let's make the choice to trust Him because His plans for us are good and not evil, to give us a future and a hope.

MEMORY VERSE

SAY: This is our last week with this memory verse. Next week we'll have a new one for you to learn. Let's hear you say it together.

Jeremiah 29:11 - "For I know the plans I have for you," declares the Lord, "plans to prosper you and not to harm you, plans to give you a hope and a future."

PRAYER CIRCLES - "God With Me" Prayer
As the children learn to pray and hear God's voice, it can be helpful to give them each a notebook so they can keep track of what they hear and are praying for. Keep these notebooks in a safe place in class until you finish this curriculum. Encourage the kids to write down prayer requests they, or their peers have, on the take home sheet so they can be reminded to pray for those things during the week. For more information on this method of prayer, please look in the reference section on page 207.
- Hand each child a notebook they'll be able to use in class for the duration of this curriculum, and a pen or pencil. Tell the kids not to write in their notebooks until they are ready to write what they're hearing from the Lord.
- **Begin with Interactive Gratitude. Have the kids think of two or three things they're grateful for.** At first, they can start with things, but try to encourage them to list what they appreciate about their peers, teachers, parents, and other people they encounter every day.

GOD HAS A PLAN FOR YOU AND ME!

- **Have the kids write down what they're thankful for in the form of a prayer.** ("God, today I'm thankful for...") Have them be as specific as possible. Instead of just saying they're thankful for their parents, have them come up with a specific reason they're thankful. The more specific they can get, the better.
- **Next, have them write down what they think God would say in response to the things they're grateful for.** This might be difficult at first if the kids don't know God's character very well. You may need to explain that God will always respond to us in love, and any judgmental, hurtful, or negative thoughts that come to their minds is not from God.
- **After the Interactive Gratitude is complete, have the kids take several deep breaths.** This will help calm their minds and bodies so they can better participate in the next portion.
- **Once everyone appears calm and relaxed, have them write down some things they want to pray about.** Have them write these things down as though God were sitting next to them having a conversation with them. ("God, the bully at school is really bothering me.") To begin, it might be best to keep things simple. Have them pray for things on their radar: bullies at school, a subject in school they're struggling with, their parent's jobs, their siblings. At this point, we don't want them to go too deep until they really start understanding how to hear God's voice.
- If they have trouble coming up with subjects, give them some ideas such as praying they sleep well at night, or get up on time, or if they're willing they can pray for God to give them a desire to get to know Him. As long as the prayer is true for them they can pray about it. We don't want them to pray just to go through the motions.
- **Once they have one or two items, have them write as though God were responding to them. Begin with how God sees them.** For example, "I see you sitting in your classroom wondering what to pray about. I see how concerned you are about this issue. I see how worried you are about this."
- **Once they've written a sentence or two on that, move to "I hear you".** For example, "I hear you crying at night about this issue. I hear you telling me you want me to fix this. I hear you telling your parents how worried you are about the bully at school."
- **Next, have them write a couple sentences that start with "I understand how hard this is for you."** For example, "I understand how hard it is for you to go to school every day knowing there is a bully there, waiting." There may be some things the kids pray about that this wouldn't apply to. If that is the case, they can skip this step.
- **Next, have them write a couple of sentences that start with "I'm glad to be with you."** For example, "I'm glad to be with you right now as you tell me about this issue. I'm glad to be with you when you're crying in your bed at night. I'm glad to be with you even when you're struggling with negative emotions."

GOD HAS A PLAN FOR YOU AND ME!

- **The last writing prompt to give them is, "I can do something about what you're going through."** This one might be harder if the kids don't understand God's character. In this case, God might respond by giving us a Bible verse reminding us of His goodness, His love, His faithfulness, etc. or He might remind us of a time in our past when we got through another difficult situation. Here is an example of what He might say, "I will help you continue to see more clearly who I am and what I've been doing in your life. I am protecting you. When you're feeling scared, remember I'm with you." Remind the kids that God will only say things that are loving, kind, and compassionate.
- **Finally, if anyone wants to share what God said to them, allow them some time for this.** This is an important step, and if you are able to spend time during the week before class practicing this method, it will help the kids be more comfortable with sharing if you are able to share from your own notebook.

GOD HAS A PLAN FOR YOU AND ME AT HOME!

LESSON SUMMARY: Today we learned how to find out what God's plan for our life is. We looked at what would happen if we asked our GPS to show us how to get somewhere, but had the music up so loud we couldn't hear the directions and didn't ever look at the GPS. We wouldn't know where or when to turn. In the same way, we have to be able to hear and know God's voice in order to find out what His plan for us is. We learned how life can easily get in the way of spending time with God, so we have to plan on including Him in our day.

MEMORY VERSE: Jeremiah 29:11 - "For I know the plans I have for you," declares the Lord, "plans to prosper you and not to harm you, plans to give you a hope and a future."

IN THE CAR
- Look out the window. Talk about the things God made. Any animals you see, trees, flowers, or plants. How did God make them to work together?
- Discuss the different ways we can hear God's voice. If you aren't sure, use examples from the Bible. God spoke to people through visions, dreams, angels, prophets, and sometimes even directly like He did with Moses.
- Discuss any plans you have for the week, then consider how we are made in the image of God since God plans things, we also plan things.

AT MEALTIMES
- Thank God for providing your family with food.
- Talk about other things God provides your family with.
- Plan a family activity together as you eat. It could be something as simple as a movie with special snacks in the front room, or playing a game with "house rules".

AT BEDTIME
- Reread Matthew 6:25-34 with your parents and talk about it.
- Pick an animal or plant to research. Spend a few minutes each evening finding out how God takes care of that plant or animal. How does it grow? What does it eat? Where does it find its food?
- Thank God for giving us everything we need.

PRAYER REQUESTS:

God And Me

UNIT 2

UNIT THEME: GOD LOVES YOU AND ME!

This unit uses popular emoji's to explain God's love for us. We begin by looking at the world's view of love, versus the Bible's. The remaining lessons will teach how God loves us always, and when we feel He's become distant it's really us who've become distant. The last lesson will look at how we can share God's love with others. This is a great unit to combine with a service project. You can find service project ideas in the Resource section of this book on page 207.

Lesson 1: What is Love?

This lesson uses several hands-on activities to explain that love is a choice and not an emotion. It also looks at 1 Corinthians 13 to show what love is according to God, then discusses what all the words, such as jealously and boastful mean.

Lesson 2: God Looks at Us with Heart Eyes

This lesson uses hands-on activities and games to explain what Jesus did for us on the cross and why He always looks at us with love, even when we don't feel we deserve it.

Lesson 3: God's Love Never Changes

This lesson looks at how people and things change over time, but God never does, which means His love for us never changes.

Lesson 4: The Good Samaritan

This lesson teaches the classic story of the Good Samaritan and will help kids understand that loving others doesn't always mean loving people who look, think, or act like us.

Lesson 5: Are We Showing God's Love to Others?

This lessons is part review of the past four lessons, and gives practical steps for how we can know if we're walking in God's love.

Optional Videos For This Unit: https://bit.ly/2D4a5Xk

Angela E. Powell

GOD LOVES YOU AND ME!

SUPPLIES NEEDED

Copies of take home sheet on page 50	Cups	Lemon juice
Baking soda	Red Kool-Aid	Sugar
Water	Spoons	Measuring spoons
Napkins	Marshmallows	Paper
Video explaining jealously	Pens or pencils	Prayer Notebooks
Marshmallow test video (optional)	Kissy-Face Emoji on page 49	

LESSON 1: WHAT IS LOVE?

WELCOME

As you welcome children to class, have this question written on a white board, piece of paper, or ask the question to each child as you welcome them. Have the children find someone they don't know very well and discuss it.

Ice Breaker Question: What is the most annoying habit other people have?

GAMES

CLASSIFICATION

SUPPLIES: Paper, Pens or pencils

- Divide kids into groups of 5-6, unless you have fewer than eight in your class.
- Have the kids in each group discuss their likes, dislikes, dreams, goals, etc.
- Pass out a piece of paper and pens or pencils to each group.
- Have them classify their group into sub-groups based on the information they learn.
- Groups could be based on food, colors, or movies they like.
- Have them write down the different sub-groups and who was in those sub-groups.
- Have a discussion with them about how people make friends because of similar likes, but we also tend to leave people out of our group because they don't like things we like.
- During the lesson, refer back to the game to show how classifying people, for good or bad reasons, can make it hard to love some people.

LESSON 1: WHAT IS LOVE?

NOTE: Page 49 has large copies of the kissy-face emoji for you to print out, color, and hang around your room or pass out to the kids. You'll want to have one you can show the kids during the lesson.

God And Me

GOD LOVES YOU AND ME!

ASK: What is love?

SAY: Those are all great answers! Today we're going to look at two different definitions of love. One of them is real love, and one of them is fake love. At the end of class, you're going to decide which definition is the real one.

SAY: The first definition comes from doctors, called psychologists. Psychologists say love is an emotion like happiness or fear. Love is a chemical reaction in the brain so we can't control who, when, or why we love the people we love. If our brains don't have the right chemical reaction, we won't be able to feel love. [5]

SAY: I need your help. We're going to make a love potion to see if we can get our brains to feel love.

HANDS-ON ACTIVITY

SUPPLIES: Paper cups, Plastic spoons, Kool-Aid mix, Baking soda, Lemon juice, Water, Sugar, Measuring spoons

- Because of the baking soda, this drink won't taste very good, but that's part of the activity.
- Give each child a cup and a spoon.
- Have each child add 2 teaspoons of Kool-Aid to their cups.
- Then add 1/8 teaspoon baking soda and mix.
- Help them add 2 tablespoons of lemon juice and watch it begin to bubble.
- Add water to fill the cups.
- Add 2 tablespoons of sugar and let them mix.
- Let the kids drink their potions.

ASK: Now that you've had your love potion, how do you feel? Do you feel so much love for me, your teacher, that you'd be willing to do some really gross chores like scrubbing toilets or changing diapers in the nursery?

SAY: Oh man, I don't think our love potion worked very well. Oh well, let's take a look at our second definition of love. This definition comes from the Bible.

---

[5] Thottam, Isabel. "What is Love?" *Defining Love & the Greek's 7 Definitions | eHarmony*, Eharmony, www.eharmony.com/what-is-love/.

Angela E. Powell

GOD LOVES YOU AND ME!

READ THE WORD

Have the kids follow along as the teacher or older kids read the following verses. **1 Corinthians 13:4-7**

ASK: Can you choose to be kind? Can you choose to be patient? What about the other things listed here? Can you choose to do those things?

SAY: Yes! So one definition of love says we can't choose who we love, why we love them, or when we love them. The other says love is a lot of things we can choose to do.

ASK: When your parents or friends give you a hug, does that hug make you feel loved? Can we choose to give someone a hug?

SAY: Giving hugs is one way we show love to people. We can choose whether or not to give someone a hug, just like we can choose to be kind or mean.

HANDS-ON ACTIVITY

SUPPLIES: Marshmallows

NOTE: If you don't want to do this in class, there are videos of the marshmallow experiment online you can show. There is a link where you can find videos on the unit overview page for this unit or you can use your own.

ASK: How many of you like marshmallows?

SAY: I have a bag of marshmallows here and I'm going to give one to each of you. Now, you can choose to eat the marshmallow when I give it to you, or you can wait until I finish doing some work I need to do. When I'm done, if you've waited to eat your marshmallow, I'll give you a second marshmallow. Remember, you only get two marshmallows if you wait to eat the first one until I finish my task, but it's your choice. Eat it now, or wait.

NOTE: Don't make the children wait more than five minutes.

SAY: Great Job! Each of you made a choice. You either chose to eat your one marshmallow, or you chose to wait so you could get two marshmallows. Those of you who waited chose to be patient. Now you were being patient because you wanted a second treat, but when we're patient with people, that's showing love.

God And Me

GOD LOVES YOU AND ME!

ASK: Those of you who chose not to wait, do you think you could have waited if you really wanted to?

SAY: Yes! Sometimes it can be a hard choice to make, but we can choose to do hard things. Let's make sure we know what all the words in these verses mean.

ASK: We talked about being patient and kind, but what does it mean to be jealous?

VIDEO: (Optional) Play a video that explains what jealously is.
There is a link on the overview page where you can find videos for this unit or you can use your own.

SAY: Jealousy is wanting something someone else has. You have negative feelings about the person because you can't have what they have. For example: If your best friend goes to Disneyland for their birthday you could get jealous because your parents can't afford to take you to Disneyland and your friend didn't invite you to go with.

ASK: What does it mean to be boastful?

SAY: If your best friend went to Disneyland for their birthday and came back and said, "I got to have dinner with Mickey Mouse, in Cinderella's castle and you didn't." that would be boasting.

ASK: What does it mean when it says, "Love keeps no record of being wronged"?

SAY: Basically, you don't keep track of how many times someone has been mean to you. For example, if someone at school pushed you and you fell down, then they asked to sit with you at lunch, you would keep track of wrongs if you said, "No, you pushed me earlier, I don't like you." You aren't choosing to forgive or love them.

SAY: When we choose to forgive people we can be kind to them, even though they did something hurtful.

ASK: So what do you think? Which definition of love is real and which is fake? Can we choose to love people or is love something we can't choose?

SAY: Right! It's something we choose! Now think about this: God is love. When I say, "God is love", that means God is all of the things listed in the verses we read today.

SAY: God is patient, God is kind. God is not jealous, boastful, or proud.

47

GOD LOVES YOU AND ME!

ASK: What else does it say God is, or is not?

SAY: God is not rude. God doesn't demand His own way. God doesn't get angry. God forgives us. God rejoices when the truth wins. God never gives up on us. God never loses faith in us, and God is always hopeful.

ASK: Did you know God was all of those things?

SAY: God loves you and me! **Hold up the kissy-face emoji.**

ASK: If you were going to send this emoji to your friends or parents what would you be telling them?

SAY: "I love you." Or, "I'm sending you kisses." Just like we use the kissy-face emoji to tell someone we love them, God wants us to remember He loves you and me! And He wants us to love people the way God loves us!

MEMORY VERSE
SAY: Let's say our memory verse a few times.

John 3:16 - For this is how God loved the world: He gave His one and only Son, so that everyone who believes in Him will not perish but have eternal life.

PRAYER CIRCLES - Groups
As the children are learning to pray and hear God's voice, it can be helpful to give them each a notebook where they can write down what they're hearing and keep track of what they've been praying for. Keep these notebooks in class until you finish this curriculum. Encourage the kids to write down prayer requests they, or their peers have on the take home sheet so they can be reminded to pray for those things during the week.
- Have kids get into groups of three or four with at least one older child or leader in each group.
- Have the kids share their prayer requests with the others in their group.
- Encourage each child to pray for one of the prayer requests presented.
- If no one has prayer requests or there aren't enough for everyone to pray about, give them suggestions such as, praying for a good, safe week for everyone or God would bring in more kids.
- If some groups finish before others, encourage the children to write down the prayer requests they heard in their group and/or spend time trying to hear God's voice.

God And Me

GOD LOVES YOU AND ME!

© 2019 Angela E. Powell

Angela E. Powell

GOD LOVES YOU AND ME AT HOME!

LESSON SUMMARY: Today we looked at 1 Corinthians 13:4-7 to see what God has to say about love. We looked at the world's definition of love and compared it to the Bible and did an experiment to see if we could make ourselves feel love before describing and defining what God's kind of love is.

MEMORY VERSE: John 3:16 - For this is how God loved the world: He gave His one and only Son, so that everyone who believes in Him will not perish but have eternal life.

IN THE CAR
- Talk about times you've felt loved by each member of your family.
- Ask your parents what you can do to make them feel loved.
- Talk about ways you can make people at your church feel loved.

AT MEALTIMES
- Talk about fun times you've had with your family.
- Make mealtime into a game to see who can make everyone smile the most.
- Think of someone in your church or community who could use some cheering up. Make them a meal and take it to them, or invite them over for a meal at your house.

AT BEDTIME
- Read 1 Corinthians 13 with your parents. Talk about times when you've felt loved and when you haven't.
- Pray and ask God to help you and your family love one another better.
- Talk about your favorite emoji's and what the meaning behind them is. Does anyone in your family have a different meaning for an emoji than you do?

PRAYER REQUESTS:

GOD LOVES YOU AND ME!

SUPPLIES NEEDED

Copies of take home sheet on page 60		Copies of emoji's on page 59
Tape	Paper or Foam hearts	Music
3 large jars	Labels	Marker
Water	Iodine	Bleach
Spoons	Prayer notebooks	
God washed away our sin video (optional)		

LESSON 2: GOD LOOKS AT US WITH HEART EYES

WELCOME

As you welcome children to class, have this question written on a white board, piece of paper, or ask the question to each child as you welcome them. Have the children find someone they don't know very well and discuss it.

Ice Breaker Question: If you could turn any activity into an Olympic sport, what would you have a good chance at winning a medal for?

GAME

MUSICAL HEARTS GAME

SUPPLIES: Paper or foam hearts, Tape, Marker, Music

- Before class, cut hearts out of paper or foam, or buy precut paper or foam hearts.
- Write actions on each heart. Some ideas are, "Walk like a robot", "Hop like a bunny", "Be still as a statue", or "Skip."
- Tape the hearts to the floor in a circle, with the actions face up.
- At the beginning of the game, have the kids stand on a heart. Turn some music on and have them walk on the hearts in the same direction.
- Turn the music off and have the kids read the action on their heart. When the music starts again, the kids must go around the circle doing the action on the heart they landed on.
- If you choose to use options where they have to stay where they are, they can walk around the circle like normal after you stop the music again.
- You can play until time is up, or remove a heart after each round. When a child is left standing in a gap, they are out.

Angela E. Powell

GOD LOVES YOU AND ME!

LESSON 2: GOD LOOKS AT US WITH HEART EYES

NOTE: Page 59 has large copies of the heart-eyes, angry, and sad emoji for you to print out, color and hang around your room or pass out to the kids. You'll need one of each to show the class and to play the game at the end of the lesson.

Hold up the heart eyes emoji.

ASK: If you were going to send this to your friends or family, what would you be saying to them?

SAY: "I love you so much!", or "I'm excited to hear from you because I love you!"

ASK: What emoji might you send to a friend who said something mean to you?

Hold up the angry and sad emoji.

ASK: Maybe one of these?

ASK: What emoji do you think God would send you if you said something mean to your parents?

Let the kids guess, then hold up the heart eyes emoji.

SAY: We might think God is angry with us or sad because we made a mistake, but actually, God is always looking at us with heart eyes.

Hold up the angry face.

ASK: If you made a mistake and someone looked at you like this, would you want to stay near them or get away from them?

SAY: God always wants us to come to Him no matter what. He loves us so much He did something so He could always look at us with heart eyes.

ASK: Do any of you know what He did?

SAY: Let's take a look in our Bibles.

God And Me

GOD LOVES YOU AND ME!

READ THE WORD

Have the kids follow along as the teacher or older kids read the following verse. **John 3:16**

SAY: God loved the world. That means every person on earth who has ever been born and who will ever be born! God loves you and me SO much He sacrificed His Son, Jesus, so He could look at us with heart eyes all the time.

ASK: What is sin?

SAY: Those are great answers, but to keep it simple, sin is anything that keeps us from having a relationship with God.

ASK: Do you feel like you have a better relationship with your parents when you follow the rules, spend time doing fun things together and talking to each other, or, when you're in trouble, have been grounded, or there is a lot of arguing?

SAY: Right, we have better relationships when we work together instead of doing things that make us not want to be near each other.

SAY: Before Jesus died on the cross and rose again, God saw all the sin in the world and it made an invisible wall between us and God. **Hold up the sad emoji.**

SAY: This wall of sin made God sad because God loves you and me SO much, but the wall of sin kept us apart. God wanted to change that, so He sent Jesus to die for our sins.

ASK: Is there still sin in the world?

SAY: Yes, but Jesus was perfect, a man who never sinned. His blood washes our sins away and God doesn't see our sin anymore. He sees the perfect person He created us to be. I'm going to show you what that looks like.

HANDS-ON ACTIVITY

SUPPLIES: Three clear jars, Labels, Marker, Water, Iodine, Bleach

NOTE: You'll want to prepare this before class. **If you aren't comfortable doing this activity in class, there are videos online that show this experiment.** There is a link where you can find videos on the unit overview page for this unit or you can use your own.

Angela E. Powell

GOD LOVES YOU AND ME!

Before class label the jars and write one of the following words on each: People, Sin, and Jesus.
- Fill the "People" jar half way with tap water.
- Fill the "Sin" jar half way with water and add enough iodine to make the liquid dark. Mix.
- Fill the "Jesus" jar half way with water and a quarter with bleach. Mix with a different spoon.

SAY: Remember, sin is anything that keeps us from having a relationship with God. When Adam and Eve chose to disobey God and eat the fruit on the tree, they sinned. Since then, everyone who is born, is born with sin. None of us are born perfect.

SAY: God wanted us to be perfect and pure like the liquid in this jar **(Hold up the "People" jar)** but because of sin, we look more like this: **Pour some of the liquid from the sin jar into the people jar.**

SAY: There is nothing we can do to change this. We can't be good enough, nice enough, or strong enough. This is how God saw us before Jesus died on the cross for us. **Hold up the sad face.**

SAY: It made God sad to see us like this because all the sin in our lives made it so we couldn't have a relationship with God. Before Jesus died and rose again there was no way to wash away our sin.

SAY: God can't sin. It's impossible for Him to sin. **Pour some of the "Sin" liquid into the "Jesus" jar.**

SAY: See. God can't sin and sin can't touch God. Since God loves you and me SO much, and He missed not being able to be close to us, He decided to take care of the sin problem. But there was only one way to do that. Only the blood of a person who had never sinned before could get rid of sin, but there were no perfect people on earth. His perfect Son had to die and the blood of Jesus was used to wash our sins away. **Pour some of the "Jesus" liquid into the "People" jar.**

SAY: All of us are still born with sin.

SAY: The verse we read today said, "For God so loved the world that He sent His only Son that whoever believes in Him will not die, but have everlasting life."

SAY: We are all still born with sin, but when we believe Jesus died to save us from sin, then the blood of Jesus goes to work and God sees us as the perfect and pure person He created us to be.

SAY: This is why God can look at us with heart eyes no matter what we do. Any sin we commit is washed with the blood of Jesus and God doesn't see it.

ASK: Do you think that means you can get away with doing bad things?

God And Me

GOD LOVES YOU AND ME!

SAY: No. Sin always comes with a consequence.

ASK: What happens when your parents catch you lying?

SAY: You might get grounded or have some other consequence like that, but the real consequence of lying is your parents can't trust you as much as they used to. Your parents still love you, but they'll keep a closer eye on you until you can earn that trust back. There is always a consequence for sin.

ASK: God made a way for us to be able to have a relationship with Him, but if we choose to sin, are we going to want to have a relationship with God?

SAY: No! Let's play a game to see what that looks like.

EMOJI RED LIGHT GREEN LIGHT
- Hold up the sad face emoji and the heart eyes emoji.
- Remind the kids sin is anything that keeps us from having a relationship with God. When we sin, it makes us feel bad inside. **(Hold up the sad face)** When we choose to obey God, and our parents, follow the rules, and love others, we feel good. **(Hold up the heart eyes)**
- This game is like red light, green light except when the sad face is held up, the kids have to take three **(3)** steps backward. When the heart eyes are shown they can speed walk **(not run)** to where the teacher is standing.
- As soon as one child is almost within arm's reach of the teacher, have the kids freeze and look to see where all the other kids are.
- End the game by making the following point:

SAY: All of us are going to sin as long as we're on this earth because we were born with sin. Some of us will get really close to God and have a great relationship with God just like [**Student**] is really close to me right now. There will be times when we mess up and our relationship with God won't be very close. **Hold up the sad face and have everyone take three steps back.**

ASK: But who is moving back and forth?

SAY: You are! God will always stay in one place ready to have a relationship with you. He is always looking at us with heart eyes. **Briefly hold up the heart eyes emoji, then put up the sad face emoji so the kids take three steps back.**

GOD LOVES YOU AND ME!

SAY: This sad face emoji is our enemy. Whenever you think God is looking at you like this it's Satan pointing out any sin in your life and saying, "You aren't good enough". It's a lie. Whenever we think God is sad because of what we've done, or angry at us, or we feel like God is too good and we aren't good enough, we're going to want to pull away from God. **Hold up the heart eyes emoji until all the kids have reached you.**

SAY: Because God loves you and me SO much, He sent His Son to die so He could always look at us with heart eyes.

SAY: God always looks at you with heart eyes. If you can remember that, then no matter what mistakes you make, no matter what other people say, no matter what our enemy says, we will be able to run to God instead of away from Him whenever life isn't going very well.

MEMORY VERSE

SAY: Our memory verse this month is the same one we read in our Bibles today. Let's say it together.

John 3:16 - For this is how God loved the world: He gave His one and only Son, so that everyone who believes in Him will not perish but have eternal life.

PRAYER CIRCLES - "God With Me" Prayer

As the children learn to pray and hear God's voice, it can be helpful to give them each a notebook so they can keep track of what they hear and are praying for. Keep these notebooks in a safe place in class until you finish this curriculum. Encourage the kids to write down prayer requests they, or their peers have, on the take home sheet so they can be reminded to pray for those things during the week. For more information on this method of prayer, please look in the reference section on page 207.

- Hand each child a notebook they'll be able to use in class for the duration of this curriculum, and a pen or pencil. Tell the kids not to write in their notebooks until they are ready to write what they're hearing from the Lord.
- **Begin with Interactive Gratitude. Have the kids think of two or three things they're grateful for.** At first, they can start with things, but try to encourage them to list what they appreciate about their peers, teachers, parents, and other people they encounter every day.
- **Have the kids write down what they're thankful for in the form of a prayer.** ("God, today I'm thankful for...") Have them be as specific as possible. Instead of just saying they're thankful for their parents, have them come up with a specific reason they're thankful. The more specific they can get, the better.

GOD LOVES YOU AND ME!

- **Next, have them write down what they think God would say in response to the things they're grateful for.** This might be difficult at first if the kids don't know God's character very well. You may need to explain that God will always respond to us in love, and any judgmental, hurtful, or negative thoughts that come to their minds is not from God.
- **After the Interactive Gratitude is complete, have the kids take several deep breaths.** This will help calm their minds and bodies so they can better participate in the next portion.
- **Once everyone appears calm and relaxed, have them write down some things they want to pray about.** Have them write these things down as though God were sitting next to them having a conversation with them. ("God, the bully at school is really bothering me.") To begin, it might be best to keep things simple. Have them pray for things on their radar: bullies at school, a subject in school they're struggling with, their parent's jobs, their siblings. At this point, we don't want them to go too deep until they really start understanding how to hear God's voice.
- If they have trouble coming up with subjects, give them some ideas such as praying they sleep well at night, or get up on time, or if they're willing they can pray for God to give them a desire to get to know Him. As long as the prayer is true for them they can pray about it. We don't want them to pray just to go through the motions.
- **Once they have one or two items, have them write as though God were responding to them. Begin with how God sees them.** For example, "I see you sitting in your classroom wondering what to pray about. I see how concerned you are about this issue. I see how worried you are about this."
- **Once they've written a sentence or two on that, move to "I hear you".** For example, "I hear you crying at night about this issue. I hear you telling me you want me to fix this. I hear you telling your parents how worried you are about the bully at school."
- **Next, have them write a couple sentences that start with "I understand how hard this is for you."** For example, "I understand how hard it is for you to go to school every day knowing there is a bully there, waiting." There may be some things the kids pray about that this wouldn't apply to. If that is the case, they can skip this step.
- **Next, have them write a couple of sentences that start with "I'm glad to be with you."** For example, "I'm glad to be with you right now as you tell me about this issue. I'm glad to be with you when you're crying in your bed at night. I'm glad to be with you even when you're struggling with negative emotions."

GOD LOVES YOU AND ME!

- **The last writing prompt to give them is, "I can do something about what you're going through."** This one might be harder if the kids don't understand God's character. In this case, God might respond by giving us a Bible verse reminding us of His goodness, His love, His faithfulness, etc. or He might remind us of a time in our past when we got through another difficult situation. Here is an example of what He might say, "I will help you continue to see more clearly who I am and what I've been doing in your life. I am protecting you. When you're feeling scared, remember I'm with you." Remind the kids that God will only say things that are loving, kind, and compassionate.
- **Finally, if anyone wants to share what God said to them, allow them some time for this.** This is an important step, and if you are able to spend time during the week before class practicing this method, it will help the kids be more comfortable with sharing if you are able to share from your own notebook.

GOD LOVES YOU AND ME!

© 2019 Angela E. Powell

Angela E. Powell

GOD LOVES YOU AND ME AT HOME!

LESSON SUMMARY: Today we talked about happy, sad, and angry emotions and how God can always look at us with heart eyes no matter what we've done. This is possible because of what He did on the cross, and there was an experiment shown to explain exactly what it was Jesus did for us when He died on the cross.

MEMORY VERSE: John 3:16 - For this is how God loved the world: He gave His one and only Son, so that everyone who believes in Him will not perish but have eternal life.

IN THE CAR
- Read a chapter of John out loud, then talk about it.
- Talk about the memory verse, then talk about what we give to each other to show our love to each member of our family. This doesn't have to be gifts, it can be things like time, patience, etc.
- Discuss how we can all have things going on in our lives that effect our emotions. Sometimes we may be frustrated about something, but we still love our family.

AT MEALTIMES
- Talk about what you've been reading in John.
- In your own words, tell your family why God is always able to look at us with heart eyes.
- Talk about how each person in the family reacts in different ways and why it's okay if one person needs alone time to calm down, and another needs to talk things out. Discuss ways you can help each other when experiencing different emotions.

AT BEDTIME
- Practice your memory verse.
- Pray for God to help you understand the Bible as you read through John.
- Read a chapter of John together as a family before bed and talk about it.

PRAYER REQUESTS:

God And Me

GOD LOVES YOU AND ME!

SUPPLIES NEEDED

Copies of take home sheet on page 67	Copies of emoji's on page 66	
Iron	Crayon melted on paper	Wax paper
Crayons	Cheese graters	Towel
Markers	Scissors	Blindfolds
Music	Prayer Notebooks	

LESSON 3: GOD'S LOVE NEVER CHANGES

WELCOME

As you welcome children to class, have this question written on a white board, piece of paper, or ask the question to each child as you welcome them. Have the children find someone they don't know very well and discuss it.

Ice Breaker Question: What game or movie universe would you most like to live in?

GAME

LISTEN TO THE SHEPHERD

SUPPLIES: Blindfolds, Music

- Divide the class into two groups – the sheep and the distracters.
- Take the "sheep" outside the room. Explain that they'll have to find the right path when they re-enter the room. Blindfold the sheep.
- Assign one child in the room to be the Voice of God. Place this person at the end of the room.
- The "Voice of God" should call quietly to the sheep, saying things like, "Here I am," "Come to me," "Follow this path," etc. The Voice of God tries to get the sheep to follow the "right path."
- All other children will be "distracters." Have the distracters spread out. They should try to get the sheep to come to them and get them off the "right path" by saying things like, "Come this way," "It's much more fun over here," "Come on! Hurry up!" "Buy me!" "On sale, on sale!"
- Play music to add to the distractions.
- Bring the sheep in and tell them whose voice they need to listen to. It will be hard because the distractors will be louder than the voice they need to hear. If it's too hard, give a signal to each distractor one by one to be quiet until all the sheep make it to the "Voice of God" person. If there is time, switch groups so everyone has a chance to be a sheep.

Angela E. Powell

GOD LOVES YOU AND ME!

LESSON 3: GOD'S LOVE NEVER CHANGES

NOTE: Page 66 has large copies of the smiley-face emoji for you to print out, color, and hang around your room or pass out to the kids. You'll need one of each to show the class.

You'll also want to melt a crayon to a piece of paper. It doesn't have to be fancy.

ASK: Who can tell me what love is? Who can tell me why God is able to look at us with heart eyes all the time?

Hold up a picture of a smiley-face emoji.

ASK: Who can tell me what this is?

SAY: Right, it's a smiley-face emoji.

ASK: Does anyone know what a smiley-face emoji looked like a few years ago? **Have someone draw it if they know, then hold up the picture of the colon & parenthesis smiley-face.**

ASK: Think about the past year. Have you changed at all? In what ways have you changed? Have any of you learned any bad habits like cracking your knuckles? What about good habits like eating healthy and exercising? Do you know anyone who hasn't changed at all in the last year?

SAY: No! All of us change in some way over time. In fact our moods can change several times in a day.

ASK: What about God? Do you think God changes?

SAY: Let's see what the Bible says.

READ THE WORD: Have the kids follow along as the teacher or older kids read the following verses. **Hebrews 13:8-9**

ASK: This says God never changes. What do you think that means?

ASK: Remember when we talked about the Bible's definition of love? What were some things 1 Corinthians 13 listed?

SAY: Patience, kindness, not being rude, jealous or angry. We also talked about how God is love.

GOD LOVES YOU AND ME!

ASK: Are you always patient? Are you always kind? What about your parents? Your friends?

SAY: We may be better at doing some of these things than other people but we aren't always able to be these things all the time. But God can. God is always kind. God is always patient. God is never irritable. God is never rude. God always looks at us with heart eyes. Just like it said in Hebrews 13. God never changes.

SAY: God loves you and me and He always will.

ASK: Is all change good? Is all change bad?

SAY: No, sometimes change is good and sometimes it's not. Other times change can look like a good thing but turns out to be bad, or the other way around. It looks bad, but turns out to be good. I'll show you what I mean.

Show the kids the piece of paper with the melted crayon stuck to it.

ASK: This crayon changed. Was the change good or bad? Why would the change be bad? **(Made a mess, crayon is ruined.)** Why would the change be good? **(Makes pretty art, melt it and mold it into a new crayon.)**

ASK: Have you ever struggled with a behavior, like learning to remember to raise your hand in school instead of shouting out the answer? Or remembering to put your dishes in the sink after you eat?

SAY: Sometimes we struggle to learn new things and our parents and teachers try to help us learn those things by giving us praise and consequences. If your teacher has a reward system you might lose points or stars when you forget to raise your hand. If we forget to put our dishes in the sink, we might lose electronic time in the evening. Our parents love us, but they want us to learn how to be responsible and clean up after ourselves so they give us consequences to help us learn.

SAY: God loves you and me and sometimes that means He has to let us go through some hard things in order to change us into something better.

ASK: Do you think if this crayon could talk, it would tell you that being hot enough to melt is fun?

SAY: Probably not. Change might be scary or hard, but if God is the one trying to change us then we can be sure the change is good because God loves you and me.

Angela E. Powell

GOD LOVES YOU AND ME!

SAY: I want you guys to change some crayons into beautiful pieces of art to help you remember God loves you, God never changes, but sometimes we need to change in order to become the person God created us to be.

HANDS-ON ACTIVITY

SUPPLIES: Wax paper, Cheese graters, Crayons, Iron, Old towels

- Give each child a sheet of wax paper and let the kids grate crayons onto the wax paper.
- When they're finished, give them a second sheet of wax paper to place on top of the crayon shavings.
- Place a towel under and on top of the wax paper, then iron until the two wax sheets stick together. It's likely the melted wax will leak out the sides so be sure to use old towels.
- Let the wax cool for a few minutes, then let the kids draw and cut out a simple shape from their artwork. (heart, square, rectangle, triangle).
- Have them write (or help them) "God never changes". You could also have them write "God never changes, but we do."

SAY: Sometimes our families change. Parents get divorced, new siblings come along, or step-families are made. Big changes like that can make us feel lonely, scared, or angry. But God always loves us, He's always there for us. God never leaves and never changes.

SAY: When we make a mistake we can feel scared about the possibility of getting in trouble or angry because you got in more trouble than you thought you deserved. But God is never angry with you, God always loves you and always looks at you with heart eyes.

SAY: Sometimes our parents, siblings, or friends say things that hurt us. But God is never rude, He is never mean. God is always kind and He always loves you.

SAY: God loves you and me and He never changes. So, if you're having a bad day, God will have a kind word for you if you'll listen for His voice. If you're having a good day, He wants to enjoy it with you. If you feel sad, God will comfort you if you'll let Him. If you're scared God will make you feel safe if you talk to Him. If you're angry God will listen. If you're lonely God will be a friend.

SAY: When everyone and everything around you is changing, God never changes.

ASK: You don't have to talk about them, or raise your hand if you don't want to, but are there things that scare you, make you angry, or make you feel hurt or alone?

GOD LOVES YOU AND ME!

SAY: I want to encourage you to pray about those things during our prayer time today. If you aren't comfortable praying with the other kids, come talk to me or another teacher and we'll pray with you.

NOTE: You may want to go right to Prayer Circles after this lesson and do the Memory Verse at the end of class.

MEMORY VERSE
SAY: Let's say our memory verse a few times.

John 3:16 - For this is how God loved the world: He gave His one and only Son, so that everyone who believes in Him will not perish but have eternal life.

PRAYER CIRCLES - Groups
As the children are learning to pray and hear God's voice, it can be helpful to give them each a notebook where they can write down what they're hearing and keep track of what they've been praying for. Keep these notebooks in class until you finish this curriculum. Encourage the kids to write down prayer requests they, or their peers have on the take home sheet so they can be reminded to pray for those things during the week.

- Have kids get into groups of three or four with at least one older child or leader in each group.
- Have the kids share their prayer requests with the others in their group.
- Encourage each child to pray for one of the prayer requests presented.
- If no one has prayer requests or there aren't enough for everyone to pray about, give them suggestions such as, praying for a good, safe week for everyone or God would bring in more kids.
- If some groups finish before others, encourage the children to write down the prayer requests they heard in their group and/or spend time trying to hear God's voice.

Angela E. Powell

GOD LOVES YOU AND ME!

© 2019 Angela E. Powell

GOD LOVES YOU AND ME AT HOME!

LESSON SUMMARY: Today we learned how everything around us changes, but God never does. We reviewed what the Bible says about love in 1 Corinthians 13 and explained how we can be changeful but God never is. Sometimes we are patient and other times we aren't, but God isn't like that, God is always patient, always kind, and He always loves us and never changes.

MEMORY VERSE: John 3:16 - For this is how God loved the world: He gave His one and only Son, so that everyone who believes in Him will not perish but have eternal life.

IN THE CAR
- Discuss how you felt about different things that happened during the day or how you expect you'll feel about certain things that are going to happen during the week.
- If anything is making you sad, angry, nervous, or any other negative emotion, pray about those things.
- Talk about changes you've seen in each of your family members over time. This could include things like, height, foot size, appetite, skills learned, etc.

AT MEALTIMES
- Talk about why emotions aren't bad, but what you do with them can be.
- If anything has upset you during the day, discuss it with your family and have them pray for you. Likewise, if anyone in your family has been upset, ask them about it and pray for them.
- Discuss skills that have been hard to learn and how those difficulties were, or are being, overcome.

AT BEDTIME
- Tell God about your day. Tell Him about things that made you happy, sad, angry, nervous, or any other emotion you had. You don't have to ask for anything, just tell Him how you felt about the day.
- Practice your memory verse.
- Ask God to show you how you've grown in the last year physically, mentally, and spiritually.

PRAYER REQUESTS:

Angela E. Powell

GOD LOVES YOU AND ME!

> **SUPPLIES NEEDED**
> Copies of take home sheet on page 74
> Cups filled with water
> Prayer Notebooks
> Copies of emoji's on page 73
> Reusable wrap bandages or strips of cloth

LESSON 4: THE GOOD SAMARITAN

WELCOME

As you welcome children to class, have this question written on a white board, piece of paper, or ask the question to each child as you welcome them. Have the children find someone they don't know very well and discuss it.

Ice Breaker Question: What do you wish you knew more about?

GAME

THE GOOD SAMARITAN GAME

> **SUPPLIES:** Reusable wrap bandages or strips of cloth, Cups of water

- Divide the kids into teams of 3-4.
- Give each team 4 wrap bandages or strips of cloth and a cup of water.
- Have each team choose someone to be the injured person and have the injured person sit on the floor on the opposite side of the room.
- When you say, "Go", each team must run to their injured person. Wrap a bandage on each arm and leg, give the injured person a drink of water, then carry them back to the starting line.
- The first group to complete all tasks, wins.

LESSON 4: THE GOOD SAMARITAN

NOTE: Page 73 has large copies of the thumbs-up emoji for you to print out, color and hang around your room, or pass out to the kids. You'll want one to show the kids during the lesson.

SAY: We've spent a lot of time discussing what God's love looks like and how He loves us. Today we'll find out how we can show God's love to the people around us, and *who* we should show God's love to.

ASK: Without using words, how do we say, "Good job!" to someone?

SAY: Those are all great ways to say, "Good job!" without using words. We're going to focus on this one. **Hold up the thumbs up emoji, or give the kids a thumbs up.**

God And Me

GOD LOVES YOU AND ME!

SAY: During today's lesson, I want you to listen for things that show God's love and things that don't. Whenever God's love is shown, or talked about, I want you to give a thumbs up. Whenever God's love is not shown or talked about, I want you to give a thumbs down.

SAY: Let's practice. I'm going to say something that is either loving or not loving.
- I only like kids who have brown hair. **(Thumbs down)**
- Every one of you is a unique and special treasure to me and God. **(Thumbs up.)**

SAY: Good, now we're going to look at a story in the Bible. Whenever something happens that looks like God's love, thumbs up. Whenever something happens that doesn't look like God's love, thumbs down.

READ THE WORD
Have the kids follow along as the teacher or older kids read the following verses. **Luke 10:25-37**

If thumbs aren't going up or down you can stop after the following verses and ask the kids if they think love is shown or not. 25, 27, 30, 31, 32, and 33.

SAY: In our story it said a Samaritan helped the injured man, but a priest and a Levite passed him by.

ASK: Why is it important to know who these people were? If I changed the people to a Pastor, a Sunday school teacher, and a bully, how would that change the story for you?

SAY: For example, what if instead of a priest and a Levite passing the man by, it was the pastor of our church and me or one of the other Sunday school teachers who passed you by and the person who helped the injured person was the biggest bully at your school.

ASK: How would you react to that story?

SAY: Knowing who the people are in the story, can help us understand it better. Back when Jesus was on the earth they had priests who worked in the temple. The temple was like the church, so the priest was like the pastor.

ASK: If you were injured and the pastor of our church saw you, but kept walking instead of helping you, how would that make you feel? **(Thumbs down)**

SAY: You would probably feel angry and upset because pastors are supposed to teach us how to love people the way God loves people.

Angela E. Powell

GOD LOVES YOU AND ME!

SAY: The second person who walked by was a Levite. The Levites were given a special job by God. Their job was to work in the temple with the priests and make sure the temple was kept clean, the rules were followed, and they did maintenance on things to make sure everything looked nice and worked the way it was supposed to. Today a Levite would be like anyone who serves in the church like me and the other Sunday school teachers, the ushers, those who clean the church during the week, and the people who work in the office.

ASK: How would you feel if I saw one of you badly hurt and walked by without helping you? **(Thumbs down)**

ASK: Does anyone know who the Samaritans were?

SAY: The Samaritans and the Israelites didn't like each other. The Samaritans are Jews just like the Israelites, but several hundred years before Jesus was born, the Israelites lost a war and many of the people were taken captive and forced to be slaves.

SAY: After some time passed, the Israelites were set free, but their land had been taken over by other people. The Samaritans didn't want to start another war in order to get their land back and wanted all the Israelites to live with and marry the people who took over their land. But God had told the Israelites not to live with or marry people from other nations. This caused the rest of the Israelites to be angry with the Samaritans. They were enemies from that point on.

SAY: So in our story, the Samaritan who helped the injured man was actually the man's enemy. Today, that would be like the meanest bully in your school helping you if you were injured. **(Thumbs up.)**

ASK: Who is Jesus telling us to show love to in this story? Are we only supposed to be kind to our friends and family?

SAY: No, we're supposed to be kind to every person we talk to. The principal at our school, our teachers, the janitor, our friends, the weird kids, the cool kids, and even the mean kids.

SAY: That can be really hard to do and none of us will ever be perfect at it because we're human.

ASK: How do we get better at being kind to all types of people?

SAY: Practicing is a good way. Another way is to have friends who choose to practice kindness so we have someone to practice with.

God And Me

GOD LOVES YOU AND ME!

ASK: Do you think you can all do that? Can you be friends who encourage others to be kind?

SAY: Another way to get better at being kind is to spend time with the one who is love.

ASK: Who is love?

SAY: God! The more time we spend with God, the more His love will rub off on us and we will start acting more like Him. Just like we start acting like our friends when we spend time with them.

MEMORY VERSE
SAY: Let's say our memory verse a few times.

John 3:16 - For this is how God loved the world: He gave His one and only Son, so that everyone who believes in Him will not perish but have eternal life.

PRAYER CIRCLES - "God With Me" Prayer
As the children learn to pray and hear God's voice, it can be helpful to give them each a notebook so they can keep track of what they hear and are praying for. Keep these notebooks in a safe place in class until you finish this curriculum. Encourage the kids to write down prayer requests they, or their peers have, on the take home sheet so they can be reminded to pray for those things during the week. For more information on this method of prayer, please look in the reference section on page 207.

- Hand each child a notebook they'll be able to use in class for the duration of this curriculum, and a pen or pencil. Tell the kids not to write in their notebooks until they are ready to write what they're hearing from the Lord.
- **Begin with Interactive Gratitude. Have the kids think of two or three things they're grateful for.** At first, they can start with things, but try to encourage them to list what they appreciate about their peers, teachers, parents, and other people they encounter every day.
- **Have the kids write down what they're thankful for in the form of a prayer.** ("God, today I'm thankful for...") Have them be as specific as possible. Instead of just saying they're thankful for their parents, have them come up with a specific reason they're thankful. The more specific they can get, the better.
- **Next, have them write down what they think God would say in response to the things they're grateful for.** This might be difficult at first if the kids don't know God's character very well. You may need to explain that God will always respond to us in love, and any judgmental, hurtful, or negative thoughts that come to their minds is not from God.
- **After the Interactive Gratitude is complete, have the kids take several deep breaths.** This will help calm their minds and bodies so they can better participate in the next portion.

GOD LOVES YOU AND ME!

- **Once everyone appears calm and relaxed, have them write down some things they want to pray about.** Have them write these things down as though God were sitting next to them having a conversation with them. ("God, the bully at school is really bothering me.") To begin, it might be best to keep things simple. Have them pray for things on their radar: bullies at school, a subject in school they're struggling with, their parent's jobs, their siblings. At this point, we don't want them to go too deep until they really start understanding how to hear God's voice.
- If they have trouble coming up with subjects, give them some ideas such as praying they sleep well at night, or get up on time, or if they're willing they can pray for God to give them a desire to get to know Him. As long as the prayer is true for them they can pray about it. We don't want them to pray just to go through the motions.
- **Once they have one or two items, have them write as though God were responding to them. Begin with how God sees them.** For example, "I see you sitting in your classroom wondering what to pray about. I see how concerned you are about this issue. I see how worried you are about this."
- **Once they've written a sentence or two on that, move to "I hear you".** For example, "I hear you crying at night about this issue. I hear you telling me you want me to fix this. I hear you telling your parents how worried you are about the bully at school."
- **Next, have them write a couple sentences that start with "I understand how hard this is for you."** For example, "I understand how hard it is for you to go to school every day knowing there is a bully there, waiting." There may be some things the kids pray about that this wouldn't apply to. If that is the case, they can skip this step.
- **Next, have them write a couple of sentences that start with "I'm glad to be with you."** For example, "I'm glad to be with you right now as you tell me about this issue. I'm glad to be with you when you're crying in your bed at night. I'm glad to be with you even when you're struggling with negative emotions."
- **The last writing prompt to give them is, "I can do something about what you're going through."** This one might be harder if the kids don't understand God's character. In this case, God might respond by giving us a Bible verse reminding us of His goodness, His love, His faithfulness, etc. or He might remind us of a time in our past when we got through another difficult situation. Here is an example of what He might say, "I will help you continue to see more clearly who I am and what I've been doing in your life. I am protecting you. When you're feeling scared, remember I'm with you." Remind the kids that God will only say things that are loving, kind, and compassionate.
- **Finally, if anyone wants to share what God said to them, allow them some time for this.** This is an important step, and if you are able to spend time during the week before class practicing this method, it will help the kids be more comfortable with sharing if you are able to share from your own notebook.

GOD LOVES YOU AND ME!

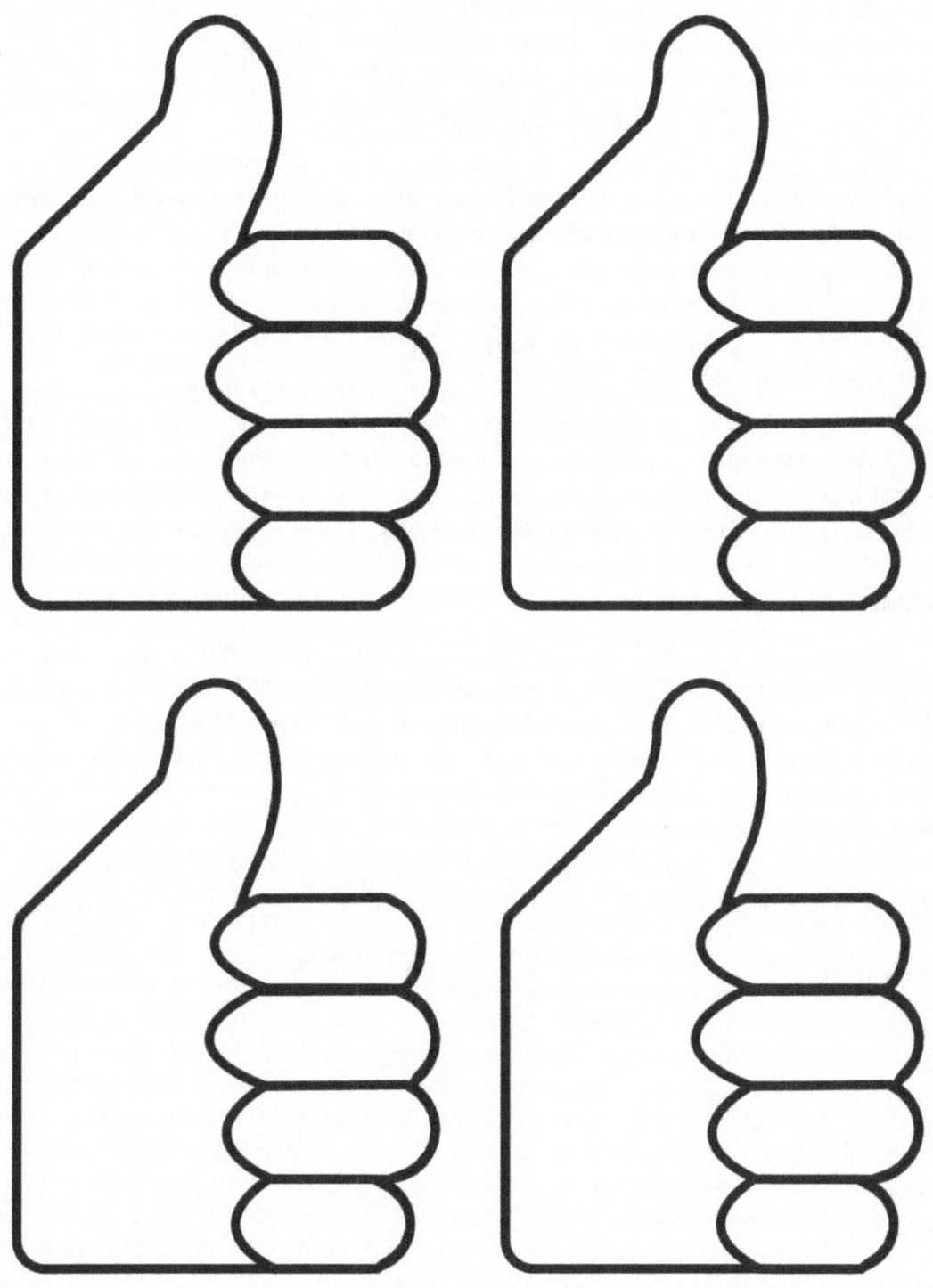

Angela E. Powell

GOD LOVES YOU AND ME AT HOME!

LESSON SUMMARY: Today we looked at the story of the Good Samaritan. The kids got to practice identifying loving behavior versus non-loving behaviors by giving a thumbs up or thumbs down throughout the story. We also made the story relevant to the kids by explaining who the priest, Levite, and Samaritan were to the injured man, substituting a Pastor, Sunday school teacher, and school bully in place of the characters to help the children understand the context.

MEMORY VERSE: John 3:16 - For this is how God loved the world: He gave His one and only Son, so that everyone who believes in Him will not perish but have eternal life.

IN THE CAR
- Brainstorm ways you can show love to other people.
- Talk about why it's important to love people the way God loves people.
- In the story of the Good Samaritan, the Samaritan has to leave and attend to business, but pays the hotel manager to care for the injured man and promises to return and pay anything more that is required. Discuss what might have happened if the Samaritan hadn't kept his promise. Why is it important to keep our promises and how is this showing love to people?

AT MEALTIMES
- Have everyone agree to make an effort to love people more this week.
- Talk about how you've already been loving people and ways you can improve.
- Talk about how you were able to love people better as the week goes on.

AT BEDTIME
- Practice your memory verse.
- Talk about ways you loved people during the day, and areas where it was a struggle.
- Reread 1 Corinthians 13:4-7 to remind each other how to love people like God loves us.

PRAYER REQUESTS:

God And Me

GOD LOVES YOU AND ME!

SUPPLIES NEEDED
Copies of take home sheet on page 80
Paper   Pens or pencils
Prayer Notebooks

Copies of emoji's on page 49
God washes away sin video (optional)

LESSON 5: ARE WE SHOWING GOD'S LOVE TO OTHERS?
WELCOME
As you welcome children to class, have this question written on a white board, piece of paper, or ask the question to each child as you welcome them. Have the children find someone they don't know very well and discuss it.

Ice Breaker Question: What are some small things that make your day better?

GAME
TELEPHONE PICTIONARY

SUPPLIES: Paper, Pens or pencils

- Before class, take several pieces of paper and fold them accordion style. Make sure each paper has the same number of folds. Make enough for each child to have one.
- Give each child a pen and paper. Have them write their name and a simple sentence on the top fold. Make sure they keep it appropriate.
- The kids will then pass their paper to the right or left, whichever you choose. The child who gets the paper will read the sentence, then in the next section, they'll draw a picture that shows what the sentence is about. When they're done, they'll fold the paper over, so their picture can be seen, but the sentence can't.
- Have the kids pass the paper again. The next child will write a sentence based on the picture the previous child drew, then fold the paper so only their sentence can be seen before passing it to the next child.
- Each fold will alternate between a picture and a sentence.
- When the bottom of the paper is reached, have the kids open up the page and read the first sentence to see if the message stayed the same. The kids can pass their papers back to each other and they can take them home.

LESSON 5: ARE WE SHOWING GOD'S LOVE TO OTHERS?

NOTE: Page 49 has large copies of the kissy-face emoji for you to print out, color, and hang around your room or pass out to the kids. You'll want one to show during class.
Hold up the kissy-face emoji.

Angela E. Powell

GOD LOVES YOU AND ME!

SAY: We used this emoji in our first lesson on God's love.

ASK: If you were going to send this to your friends or family, what would you be telling them?

SAY: "I love you," or "I'm sending you kisses."

SAY: Just like we use emoji's to remind people we love them, God wants us to remember He loves you and me.

ASK: But how do we know if we're really loving people the way God wants us to?

SAY: We could look at the verses and Bible stories we've read in the past four weeks and remind ourselves what God's love looks like, but there are a lot of stories and verses in the Bible that give us an even better idea of how we can love people and how God loves us.

SAY: Today we're going to look at part of a letter John wrote. John was a very close friend of Jesus when He was on the earth. John is known as "The Disciple Whom Jesus Loved."

ASK: Do you think John had that title because Jesus loved John more than He loved the other eleven disciples?

SAY: No! John had a better understanding of God's love than the other disciples did and because of this, John and Jesus had a closer friendship. All of the disciples could have called themselves the disciple whom Jesus loved. In fact, we can all say that about ourselves.

SAY: I am the teacher whom Jesus loves. [Child's Name] is the child whom Jesus loves.

SAY: Let's see what John has to tell us about God's love.

READ THE WORD
Have the kids follow along as the teacher or older kids read the following verses. **1 John 4:7-21 (The Message translation may make this easier for the kids to understand and is the version used in quotes throughout this lesson.)**

SAY: These verses can be a little confusing, so let's break it into sections and see if we can understand what John is trying to say.

God And Me

GOD LOVES YOU AND ME!

ASK: Verse 7 tells us to keep loving each other. That's pretty easy to understand right?

SAY: The next couple of verses say anyone who loves God is born of God, but if we refuse to love people, then we don't know anything about God because God is love.

ASK: What does that mean?

SAY: John gives us a clue in the next thing he says. He reminds us God sent His Son, Jesus, to die for us because He loved us so much. John tells us this is how God showed us He loved us. We talked about this when we used the heart-eyes emoji.

ASK: Does anyone know how we invite Jesus into our lives?

SAY: We choose to believe Jesus died on the cross for our sins and rose again three days later. We ask Him to come into our lives and be a part of us because we believe He loved us so much He died to save us from sin.

ASK: Who remembers the activity we did **(Or video we watched)** to show how Jesus' blood washed our sins away?

Optional: Show a video of the science experiment using iodine, bleach and water to remind the kids. There is a link on the overview page where you can find videos for this unit or you can use your own.

SAY: When John says anyone who loves is born of God, He's saying if we've accepted Jesus as our Lord and Savior, we're going to choose to love people. When we first get saved, we may not always choose to love people because we're just starting to get to know God.

SAY: John starts the next section with, "This is how we know we're living in Him and God is living in us." He says a lot of things after that, but the point we want to look at is in verses 15-16.

SAY: It says anyone who confesses that Jesus is the son of God participates continuously in an intimate relationship with God. Then it says, we believe Jesus is the Son of God so much, we've embraced God's love with all our heart and soul.

ASK: What does that mean? What does it mean to "participate continuously"?

Angela E. Powell

GOD LOVES YOU AND ME!

SAY: It means you're doing something all the time. In this case, it means you're always in relationship with God. You make Him part of every area of your life.

SAY: The next section I want to look at is the part that says, "love banishes fear".

ASK: What do you think that means?

SAY: When we understand God's love, we're going to realize how powerful God's love is. Sometimes we don't say things to our friends because we're afraid they'll get mad at us, or won't want to be our friend anymore. But when we understand God's love, we won't be afraid to say something if we're saying it because we love that person.

SAY: The last part of this chapter in 1 John reminds us of God's commandment for us to love one another. John says, "Loving God includes loving people. You've got to love both."

ASK: What does that mean?

SAY: When we understand God's love for us, we'll want to love other people just like He loves us.

ASK: How many of you love God? Do you think you understand God's love a little better now?

SAY: Great, let's do our best to show everyone we know how much God loves them this week.

MEMORY VERSE
SAY: Let's say our memory verse a few times.

John 3:16 - For this is how God loved the world: He gave His one and only Son, so that everyone who believes in Him will not perish but have eternal life.

PRAYER CIRCLES - Groups
As the children are learning to pray and hear God's voice, it can be helpful to give them each a notebook where they can write down what they're hearing and keep track of what they've been praying for. Keep these notebooks in class until you finish this curriculum. Encourage the kids to write down prayer requests they, or their peers have on the take home sheet so they can be reminded to pray for those things during the week.
- Have kids get into groups of three or four with at least one older child or leader in each group.
- Have the kids share their prayer requests with the others in their group.

GOD LOVES YOU AND ME!

- Encourage each child to pray for one of the prayer requests presented.
- If no one has prayer requests or there aren't enough for everyone to pray about, give them suggestions such as, praying for a good, safe week for everyone or God would bring in more kids.
- If some groups finish before others, encourage the children to write down the prayer requests they heard in their group and/or spend time trying to hear God's voice.

Angela E. Powell

GOD LOVES YOU AND ME AT HOME!

LESSON SUMMARY: Today we looked at 1 John 4:7-21 to learn more about how to love others. We saw that it's important to have an ongoing relationship with Jesus in order to love people the way Jesus wants us to love them.

MEMORY VERSE: John 3:16 - For this is how God loved the world: He gave His one and only Son, so that everyone who believes in Him will not perish but have eternal life.

IN THE CAR
- Brainstorm ways you can show love to other people.
- Talk about why it's important to love people the way God loves people.
- Discuss why it's important to have a relationship with Jesus so we can learn from Him how to love others. Discuss how we have a relationship with Jesus.

AT MEALTIMES
- Have everyone agree to make an effort to love people more this week.
- Talk about how you've already been loving people and ways you can improve.
- Talk about how you were able to love people better as the week goes on.

AT BEDTIME
- Practice your memory verse.
- Talk about ways you loved people during the day, and areas where it was a struggle.
- Reread 1 Corinthians 13:4-7 to remind each other how to love people like God loves us.
- Pray and ask God to help you love people the way He wants you to love them.

PRAYER REQUESTS:

God And Me

UNIT 3

UNIT THEME: GOD SAVED YOU AND ME!

Each lesson in this unit uses eggs in some form to explain the Resurrection story. If your church has a kitchen, you may want to keep a carton in the fridge for your teachers. This unit breaks down the Resurrection story into five lessons and explains the events leading up to Jesus' death and resurrection so the children have a better understanding of the impact of His sacrifice for us. **While these lessons talk about the Easter story, they do not have to be used exclusively at Easter.**

Lesson 1: Palm Sunday - Celebrating Jesus
This lesson teaches about Palm Sunday. It looks at the reason people were celebrating, or honoring, Jesus. We define what it means to honor people and the various ways we do that through celebrations.

Lesson 2: The Last Supper - Celebrating Passover
In this lesson we give a brief overview of the Passover holiday, why it was, and still is, celebrated by the Jewish people and what each of the elements on a Seder plate represents. We also learn how each of those elements points to Jesus and what He did on the cross.

Lesson 3: The Garden - Jesus Prays
This lesson talks about temptation and how prayer can help us when we're feeling tempted. We take a look at the time Jesus spent praying in the garden before He was arrested and show how Jesus was able to remain calm and resist temptation, but the disciples, who chose to sleep instead of pray, fled, fought, and gave into temptation.

Lesson 4: Good Friday - Jesus Dies
In this lesson we talk about what happens when we feel big emotions. We look at how various people acted when they were dealing with big emotions after Jesus was arrested and when He was put on the cross. Then we look at what Jesus did. This lesson also includes some hands-on tips on how kids can calm their big emotions.

Lesson 5: Resurrection Sunday - Jesus is Alive!
In this lesson we talk about whether we really believe in Jesus or if we just know about Him. We look at the resurrection story to see Jesus' disciples knew Jesus told them He would rise from the dead after three days, but they didn't really believe it. We also talk about ways the kids can find out, and make a decision for themselves about the Bible and Jesus and are invited to accept Him as their Savior.

Optional Videos For This Unit: https://bit.ly/2TcmOAa

Angela E. Powell

GOD SAVED YOU AND ME!

SUPPLIES NEEDED

Copies of take home sheet on page 87
Deviled eggs (optional)
Small paper cups
Jelly beans
Popsicle sticks
Prayer Notebooks
How to make deviled eggs video (optional)

LESSON 1: PALM SUNDAY – CELEBRATING JESUS

WELCOME

As you welcome children to class, have this question written on a white board, piece of paper, or ask the question to each child as you welcome them. Have the children find someone they don't know very well and discuss it.

Ice Breaker Question: What one thing do you really want, but can't afford?

GAME

JELLY BEAN PARTY

SUPPLIES: Small paper cups, Jelly beans, Popsicle sticks

- Give each child a little cup filled with jelly beans and a Popsicle stick.
- When you say "Go" the kids must put one end of the Popsicle stick into their mouth and attempt to balance four jelly beans on it.
- As an alternative, you can have teams of two. One puts the Popsicle stick in their mouth, the other tries to balance the jelly beans on the stick.
- Feel free to alter the number of jelly beans they have to balance based on the age group. If you have a lot of older kids, you may want to increase the amount to six. For younger children, you may want to start with two.

LESSON 1: PALM SUNDAY – CELEBRATING JESUS

NOTE: Prepare deviled eggs in advance OR have images OR a video of how deviled eggs are made ready to show the kids. Be aware of any food allergies before serving to the kids. There is a link where you can find videos on the unit overview page for this unit or you can use your own.

ASK: If you could have any celebrity or famous person stay at your house for one whole day, who would you want it to be and why?

GOD SAVED YOU AND ME!

ASK: If this celebrity called you up and said, "Hey, I'm coming to your house today, I'll see you in an hour." What would you do? How would you get ready for their visit? Would you clean your house? Find out their favorite meal and make it? How would you want to spend your day? Playing video games? Showing them around your city?

SAY: Jesus was a celebrity. He went around teaching people about God, but in a new way. He also did miracles like healing sick people and doing a lot of good things. Many people liked listening to Jesus talk so they would follow Him around. Kind of like some people will go to every concert when a certain singer or band comes to town.

SAY: Some people followed Jesus because they needed healing or wanted to see someone get healed. For them, it was like going to a magic show or going to see a celebrity in hopes of getting their autograph. Other people followed Him because they didn't like Jesus and wanted to get Him in trouble. They were looking for proof that Jesus was only pretending to heal people, or He was trying to teach them wrong things. Like people who work for magazines who like to spread mean rumors about celebrities.

SAY: One day, Jesus went to Jerusalem. His disciples didn't want Him to go there because the city leaders were looking for a way to arrest Jesus, but it was almost time for Passover, a very special celebration that Jewish people still celebrate today, and Jesus wanted to be there for it.

SAY: The disciples may not have been too happy that Jesus wanted to go to Jerusalem, but His fans were excited when they heard Jesus was coming. Let's read the Bible and find out what they did when Jesus came to town.

READ THE WORD
Have the kids follow along as the teacher or older kids read the following verses. **Luke 19:35-40**

ASK: Why are celebrities so special? Why do we get so excited about them?

SAY: We might admire their acting or musical skills, or it could be all our friends know who that person is and we're excited because so few people ever get to meet a celebrity. In other words, we could say it's an honor to meet them.

ASK: Do you know what the word 'honor' means?

GOD SAVED YOU AND ME!

SAY: It means we respect or admire them. We could also say we hold them in a place of honor, or importance in our lives. When we honor someone, we're telling them they're important and special to us.

SAY: The people who liked Jesus wanted to honor him, but they didn't have time to plan anything so they danced and sang in the street as He walked by. They took their coats off and cut down palm branches and laid them in the road. It was their version of laying out a red carpet for Jesus. We celebrate Easter to honor what God did for us when He died on the cross and rose again.

ASK: What other holidays do we celebrate to honor God or people?

SAY: We celebrate Martin Luther King Jr. day to honor his work in the civil rights movement. Christmas is a time to celebrate the birth of Jesus. On Valentine's Day we honor those we love by reminding them how much we love them. On Independence Day we honor people in our military who sacrifice so much to keep our country safe. We also celebrate birthdays to show people we're glad they were born.

ASK: Many of these celebrations feel like a party don't they? And many parties have food, right? What kind of foods do you like to have at a party?

ASK: Those are all great answers! What do we do with the eggs on Easter? What kind of party food can you make with eggs?

SAY: Great answers! A lot of people like to have deviled eggs at a party.

ASK: Have you ever had a deviled egg?

NOTE: If you made deviled eggs, let the kids try one if they want. Again, be aware of food allergies. If you did not bring eggs, show pictures or a video of how deviled eggs are made. There is a link on the overview page where you can find videos for this unit or you can use your own.

ASK: Why do you think the people got so excited about Jesus coming to town?

SAY: He healed people and taught them things, and they believed God had sent Jesus to save them.

ASK: If I told you someone was going to come save us, what would you think? What would we need to be saved from?

God And Me

GOD SAVED YOU AND ME!

SAY: The Jewish people thought Jesus was going to get a great army together and defeat the Roman Empire so the Jews could have Israel all to themselves again.

ASK: But is that what happened?

SAY: No, when Jesus said He came to save the people, He was talking about saving us from sin. But on Palm Sunday, the people were shouting, singing, and having a party for Jesus. As we go through the rest of these lessons about the Resurrection, we're going to find out how quickly the people changed their minds about how wonderful Jesus was, and why.

MEMORY VERSE

SAY: Let's say our memory verse a few times.

Romans 8:11 – The Spirit of God, who raised Jesus from the dead, lives in you. And just as God raised Jesus Christ from the dead, He will give life to your mortal bodies by this same Spirit living within you.

PRAYER CIRCLES - "God With Me" Prayer

As the children learn to pray and hear God's voice, it can be helpful to give them each a notebook so they can keep track of what they hear and are praying for. Keep these notebooks in a safe place in class until you finish this curriculum. Encourage the kids to write down prayer requests they, or their peers have, on the take home sheet so they can be reminded to pray for those things during the week. For more information on this method of prayer, please look in the reference section on page 207.

- Hand each child a notebook they'll be able to use in class for the duration of this curriculum, and a pen or pencil. Tell the kids not to write in their notebooks until they are ready to write what they're hearing from the Lord.
- **Begin with Interactive Gratitude. Have the kids think of two or three things they're grateful for.** At first, they can start with things, but try to encourage them to list what they appreciate about their peers, teachers, parents, and other people they encounter every day.
- **Have the kids write down what they're thankful for in the form of a prayer.** ("God, today I'm thankful for...") Have them be as specific as possible. Instead of just saying they're thankful for their parents, have them come up with a specific reason they're thankful. The more specific they can get, the better.
- **Next, have them write down what they think God would say in response to the things they're grateful for.** This might be difficult at first if the kids don't know God's character very well. You may need to explain that God will always respond to us in love, and any judgmental, hurtful, or negative thoughts that come to their minds is not from God.

GOD SAVED YOU AND ME!

- **After the Interactive Gratitude is complete, have the kids take several deep breaths.** This will help calm their minds and bodies so they can better participate in the next portion.
- **Once everyone appears calm and relaxed, have them write down some things they want to pray about.** Have them write these things down as though God were sitting next to them and having a conversation with them. ("God, the bully at school is really bothering me.") To begin, it might be best to keep things simple. Have them pray for things on their radar: bullies at school, a subject in school they're struggling with, their parent's jobs, their siblings. At this point, we don't want them to go too deep until they really start understanding how to hear God's voice.
- If they have trouble coming up with subjects, give them some ideas such as praying they sleep well at night, or get up on time, or if they're willing they can pray for God to give them a desire to get to know Him. As long as the prayer is true for them they can pray about it. We don't want them to pray just to go through the motions.
- **Once they have one or two items, have them write as though God were responding to them. Begin with how God sees them.** For example, "I see you sitting in your classroom wondering what to pray about. I see how concerned you are about this issue. I see how worried you are about this."
- **Once they've written a sentence or two on that, move to "I hear you".** For example, "I hear you crying at night about this issue. I hear you telling me you want me to fix this. I hear you telling your parents how worried you are about the bully at school."
- **Next, have them write a couple sentences that start with "I understand how hard this is for you."** For example, "I understand how hard it is for you to go to school every day knowing there is a bully there, waiting." There may be some things the kids pray about that this wouldn't apply to. If that is the case, they can skip this step.
- **Next, have them write a couple of sentences that start with "I'm glad to be with you."** For example, "I'm glad to be with as you tell me about this issue. I'm glad to be with you when you're crying at night. I'm glad to be with you when you're struggling with negative emotions."
- **The last writing prompt to give them is, "I can do something about what you're going through."** This one might be harder if the kids don't understand God's character. In this case, God might respond by giving us a Bible verse reminding us of His goodness, His love, His faithfulness, etc. or He might remind us of a time in our past when we got through another difficult situation. Here is an example of what He might say, "I will help you continue to see more clearly who I am and what I've been doing in your life. When you feel scared, remember I'm with you." Remind the kids God will only say things that are loving, kind, and compassionate.
- **Finally, if anyone wants to share what God said to them, allow them some time for this.** This is an important step, and if you are able to spend time during the week before class practicing this method, it will help the kids be more comfortable with sharing if you are able to share from your own notebook.

GOD SAVED YOU AND ME AT HOME!

LESSON SUMMARY: Today we learned Palm Sunday was actually a party the people threw for Jesus. They were excited about Him coming to town to teach and heal them. When they discovered He was coming to their city, they celebrated Him.

MEMORY VERSE: Romans 8:11 – The Spirit of God, who raised Jesus from the dead, lives in you. And just as God raised Jesus Christ from the dead, He will give life to your mortal bodies by this same Spirit living within you.

IN THE CAR
- Discuss different reasons we might throw a party.
- If you were going to throw a party for Jesus, what would your party look like?
- Honor is recognizing a person for who they are and what they've done. Discuss how the people honored Jesus by laying down a 'red carpet' of palm leaves and coats for him.

AT MEALTIMES
- Discuss ways we can honor, or celebrate each other.
- Discuss your plans for an upcoming holiday, birthday, or anniversary. Discuss why we celebrate these occasions.
- Discuss how it makes you feel when you celebrate someone else, and how it feels to be celebrated.

AT BEDTIME
- Practice your memory verse.
- Pray for some of the prayer requests you heard at church.
- Discuss ways you can celebrate, or honor, different people in your life. Teachers, parents, friends, pastors, Sunday school teachers, etc.

PRAYER REQUESTS:

GOD SAVED YOU AND ME!

SUPPLIES NEEDED

Copies of take home sheet on page 92	Hardboiled eggs	Seder elements (marked *)
*Horseradish	*Lettuce	*Hardboiled egg
*Applesauce	*Bone	*Crackers
Saltine crackers	Frosting	Plastic knives
Red licorice	Paper plates	Candies for decoration
Prayer Notebooks		

LESSON 2: THE LAST SUPPER – CELEBRATING PASSOVER

WELCOME

As you welcome children to class, have this question written on a white board, piece of paper, or ask the question to each child as you welcome them. Have the children find someone they don't know very well and discuss it.

Ice Breaker Question: What is the most impressive thing you know how to do?

GAME

MATZAH HOUSE

SUPPLIES: Saltine crackers, Frosting, Plastic knives, Red licorice, Paper plates, Candies for decoration

- Divide kids into groups of three or four.
- Have the kids work together to create a house from crackers, using frosting as the glue.
- Have them make a door from the red licorice.
- They can also attempt to cut crackers in half to make triangles and add the pyramids of Egypt to their creation.
- For added creativity, you can get other small candies and let them decorate their houses.
- You can refer to their creations during the lesson.

LESSON 2: THE LAST SUPPER – CELEBRATING PASSOVER

NOTE: Have hardboiled eggs prepared before class. Be aware of any food allergies before serving them to the kids.

ASK: Have you ever been to a dinner party? Maybe you went out to a special restaurant for someone's birthday, or had a BBQ in your backyard and invited some friends over?

God And Me

GOD SAVED YOU AND ME!

ASK: What do people do at a dinner party? Eat, talk, maybe play games?

SAY: Last week we talked about the party people had in the streets when Jesus went to Jerusalem for the Passover. Several days after that party in the streets, Jesus invited His twelve followers to a special dinner party to celebrate the Passover.

ASK: Does anyone know what the Passover was all about? Does anyone remember the story of Moses and the ten plagues?

SAY: The very last plague was the death of every firstborn child in Egypt. But God told the Israelites to kill and cook a lamb and brush the blood of the lamb around the doors of their home. When God came through, He "passed over" any home with blood on it, but any home that didn't have blood on it, the first born child in that home died.

SAY: After this, the Israelites were able to run away from Egypt where they had been slaves for many years. The Passover is a celebration that reminds the Jewish people how God saved them from Egypt. So that's why Jesus and His disciples were in Jerusalem, to celebrate this special holiday.

Show the kids the Seder plate you set up, or show them pictures of one. If you have samples of the different foods, you can offer to let kids have a taste. But be aware of food allergies.

SAY: I want to show you what Jesus and His followers might have eaten at that dinner party and why.

HORSERADISH
SAY: This is called horseradish. It can be really spicy. They ate this bitter food to remind them how horrible it was to be slaves in Egypt.

HARDBOILED EGG [6]
SAY: The egg represents new life. When a chick is born, it breaks out of the shell. Well, just like a hen has to sit on an egg for a while before it hatches, the Jews had to spend time wandering in the desert before they became a nation of their own.

LETTUCE
SAY: The lettuce is dipped in salt water.

---

[6] The last Supper https://www.chabad.org/holidays/passover/pesach_cdo/aid/667075/jewish/The-Egg-in-Exodus.htm

Angela E. Powell

GOD SAVED YOU AND ME!

ASK: Have you ever cried and had some of your tears drip down your face and into your mouth?

SAY: Our tears taste salty. So the lettuce dipped in salt water is to remind the Israelites of all the tears they cried when they asked God to save them from slavery in Egypt.

APPLESAUCE
SAY: The applesauce has two meanings. 1. It's sweet, which is a reminder that freedom is sweet. 2. It looks like the clay the Jews used to make bricks in Egypt, so it reminds them of all the hard work they had to do.

BONE
SAY: The bone represents the lamb they had to kill and eat and the lamb's blood they had to spread on the doors.

CRACKERS
ASK: Did you know it takes three hours to make bread?

SAY: That's a long time! But the Jews didn't have time to wait for their bread to rise and bake, they had to escape Egypt really fast, so their bread cooked flat, like a cracker. It reminds them how they had to be ready to go when God saved them.

SAY: Now, when Jesus sat at the table with His followers having this meal, He said something that surprised them. Let's read about it in the Bible and see if you can figure out what was so surprising.

READ THE WORD
Have the kids follow along as the teacher or older kids read the following verses. **Luke 22:14-20**

SAY: The Passover was supposed to remind the Jewish people of something that happened over a thousand years before Jesus came to earth. But Jesus said the meaning of the Passover hadn't happened yet.

ASK: What was Jesus talking about?

SAY: Jesus was telling His followers HE was going to die. HE was going to be the sacrifice instead of the lamb **(Show the bone again)**. Jesus was going to save us **(Show the applesauce again)** from the bitterness of sin **(Show the horseradish again)**. Because we are slaves to sin without Jesus.

GOD SAVED YOU AND ME!

SAY: Jesus told His disciples what was about to happen. This dinner party was supposed to be a celebration, but Jesus knew what was coming and it was hard for Him to celebrate. He knew He would have to go through some really hard things, but He also knew when it was over, He would be able to have a relationship with us again, and that is why He was able to celebrate the Passover. Next week we'll look at what happens right after this dinner party ends.

MEMORY VERSE

SAY: Let's say our memory verse a few times.

Romans 8:11 – The Spirit of God, who raised Jesus from the dead, lives in you. And just as God raised Jesus Christ from the dead, He will give life to your mortal bodies by this same Spirit living within you.

PRAYER CIRCLES - Groups

As the children are learning to pray and hear God's voice, it can be helpful to give them each a notebook where they can write down what they're hearing and keep track of what they've been praying for. Keep these notebooks in class until you finish this curriculum. Encourage the kids to write down prayer requests they, or their peers have on the take home sheet so they can be reminded to pray for those things during the week.

- Have kids get into groups of three or four with at least one older child or leader in each group.
- Have the kids share their prayer requests with the others in their group.
- Encourage each child to pray for one of the prayer requests presented.
- If no one has prayer requests or there aren't enough for everyone to pray about, give them suggestions such as, praying for a good, safe week for everyone or God would bring in more kids.
- If some groups finish before others, encourage the children to write down the prayer requests they heard in their group and/or spend time trying to hear God's voice.

Angela E. Powell

GOD SAVED YOU AND ME AT HOME!

LESSON SUMMARY: Today we talked about the Passover and how to represents God saving the Israelites from slavery in Egypt. We looked at the different elements on a Seder plate from a Passover table and talked about what each element means. Then we looked at the surprising thing Jesus told His disciples about Passover - the real meaning of Passover hadn't happened yet! Finally, we went over the Seder elements again to show how they pointed to what Jesus did on the cross.

MEMORY VERSE: Romans 8:11 – The Spirit of God, who raised Jesus from the dead, lives in you. And just as God raised Jesus Christ from the dead, He will give life to your mortal bodies by this same Spirit living within you.

IN THE CAR
- Discuss your favorite holidays and why they're your favorite.
- Talk about why it's important for us to remember certain events in history like Passover, Jesus' death and resurrection, or even our own birth.
- Jesus had reason to be happy about celebrating the Passover because it meant He could have a relationship with His people again, but there was also reason for Him to be sad because He had to go through a lot of pain. Discuss why some people might have a hard time with different holidays.

AT MEALTIMES
- Horseradish is part of the Seder plate as a reminder that living in Egypt as a slave was bitter and no fun. Serve horseradish at dinner one evening and let everyone try a little. Then discuss how effective horseradish is as a reminder of something bitter.
- Make a quiche or other egg dish for dinner one evening and let the kids help. Talk about the different parts of the egg, what their purpose is, and what can be done in cooking and/or gardening with the different parts.
- Have a discussion about how and why food is able to bring people together.

AT BEDTIME
- Practice your memory verse.
- Read the story of The Ten Plagues together as a family. **(Exodus Chapter 7 - Chapter 11)**
- Discuss traditions you have in your family that other families may not have.

PRAYER REQUESTS:

God And Me

GOD SAVED YOU AND ME!

> **SUPPLIES NEEDED**
> Copies of take home sheet on page 98   Hardboiled egg   Masking tape
> Old bed sheet (small) OR tug-o-war rope   Bag of bite sized candies
> Prayer Notebooks

LESSON 3: THE GARDEN – JESUS PRAYS
WELCOME

As you welcome children to class, have this question written on a white board, piece of paper, or ask the question to each child as you welcome them. Have the children find someone they don't know very well and discuss it.

Ice Breaker Question: What is the best compliment you've ever received?

GAME
CANDY TUG

> **SUPPLIES:** Old bed sheet (small) OR tug-o-war rope, Masking tape, Bag of bite sized candies

- Before class, fold the sheet in fours lengthwise. Tie a knot at each end.
- Using the masking tape, draw a line down the center of the room.
- Divide the kids, trying to even out strength on both sides for the first round.
- Have them play a game of tug-o-war with the masking tape line in the center.
- When one team is pulled over the line, that team loses.
- Have the losing team line up at one end of the masking tape line. Give them each a piece of unwrapped candy.
- The kids on the losing team must place the candy on their lips and walk along the masking tape line without dropping or tasting the candy.
- When they reach the end of the line, have them set aside their candy for later.
- Take half of the losing team and send them to the winning team and vice versa.
- Play another round. Have the losing team do the candy walk.
- Play until all kids have at least one candy or time is up.

LESSON 3: THE GARDEN – JESUS PRAYS

ASK: Has anyone ever had a mosquito bite? What happens when you have a mosquito bite? It itches right? Are you supposed to scratch a mosquito bite? Why not?

SAY: Scratching a mosquito bite creates a sore.

Angela E. Powell

GOD SAVED YOU AND ME!

ASK: Do you know what temptation is?

SAY: Temptation is the desire to do something, especially something wrong or unwise. We all know we shouldn't scratch a mosquito bite, but the desire to scratch can be really strong.

SAY: We might be tempted to eat one more piece of candy even though Mom and Dad said not to because candy is SO yummy! If our parents ask us to do the dishes or take out the trash while they're out running errands, we might be tempted to play video games instead. Then, when we hear the car pull up, we try to get the chore done before Mom or Dad come inside.

SAY: Jesus knew when He would be arrested and when He would die.

ASK: Do you think Jesus was ever tempted to say, "God, I don't want to do this, find someone else."?

SAY: The Bible tells us Jesus prayed and said, "Lord, if there is any other way to save people from sin, don't make me go through this, but if it's the only way then I'm willing to do it." Let's read about Jesus' prayer.

READ THE WORD: Have the kids follow along as the teacher or older kids read the following verses. **Luke 23:39-53**

ASK: Do you think if you knew you were going to be tortured and then die a slow, painful death, you might be afraid?

SAY: Yeah! That's why Jesus was praying. He needed some extra strength.

ASK: Why did Jesus ask His disciples to pray?

SAY: So they wouldn't give into temptation.

ASK: What kind of temptation do you think Jesus was talking about?

SAY: Jesus told His followers what was going to happen. He told them He would die and be raised from the dead three days later, but they didn't understand He was being serious. When He said He was going to die and come back to life, His disciples thought He meant something different. They didn't think He would actually die because He was their hero!

God And Me

GOD SAVED YOU AND ME!

SAY: But Jesus knew, and He also knew His followers would be scared. So He told them to pray for strength, just like Jesus was.

ASK: But what did they do instead?

SAY: They fell asleep! Let's read what happened to one of Jesus' followers.

READ THE WORD
Have the kids follow along as the teacher or older kids read the following verses. **Luke 23:54-62**

SAY: Peter was afraid he would be arrested too, so he pretended not to know Jesus. Peter gave into temptation.

ASK: Do you think Peter would have acted differently if he'd stayed awake and prayed like Jesus asked him to?

ASK: If Jesus resisted the temptation to give up because He prayed, and Peter gave into temptation when he didn't pray, what do we need to do when we're tempted?

SAY: Pray! **(Hold up a hardboiled egg)** Sometimes it can be hard to know how to pray, or what to pray for. An egg can help us remember.

ASK: What is the outside part of an egg called? What does the shell do?

SAY: The shell protects the egg. So it can remind us to pray for protection.

ASK: What kind of protection can we ask God for?

SAY: Keeping our schools, church, and neighborhoods safe. Praying for people who protect us like police, firefighters, doctors, nurses, and teachers. All of those things are outside our homes, just like the shell is the outside layer of an egg.

ASK: What is the next layer of an egg? **(Begin peeling the shell from the egg)**

SAY: The egg white. This part of the egg protects the yolk, which is each of you.

ASK: So what surrounds you that you can pray for?

GOD SAVED YOU AND ME!

SAY: Parents, friends, family, pets, and your home. You can thank God for these things.

SAY: (Peel the egg white away from the yolk) Finally, the yolk, which is you. Pray for your needs. Thank God for things He's given you. Tell God about what makes you happy, sad, angry, embarrassed, frustrated, excited, or scared.

SAY: The next time you see an egg or have eggs for breakfast you can be reminded how to pray, and what to pray for. And remember, the more we pray, the more we'll be able to resist temptation, just like Jesus did when He was arrested even though He hadn't done anything wrong.

MEMORY VERSE
SAY: Let's say our memory verse a few times.

Romans 8:11 – The Spirit of God, who raised Jesus from the dead, lives in you. And just as God raised Jesus Christ from the dead, He will give life to your mortal bodies by this same Spirit living within you.

PRAYER CIRCLES - "God With Me" Prayer
As the children learn to pray and hear God's voice, it can be helpful to give them each a notebook so they can keep track of what they hear and are praying for. Keep these notebooks in a safe place in class until you finish this curriculum. Encourage the kids to write down prayer requests they, or their peers have, on the take home sheet so they can be reminded to pray for those things during the week. For more information on this method of prayer, please look in the reference section on page 207.

- Hand each child a notebook they'll be able to use in class for the duration of this curriculum, and a pen or pencil. Tell the kids not to write in their notebooks until they are ready to write what they're hearing from the Lord.
- **Begin with Interactive Gratitude. Have the kids think of two or three things they're grateful for.** At first, they can start with things, but try to encourage them to list what they appreciate about their peers, teachers, parents, and other people they encounter every day.
- **Have the kids write down what they're thankful for in the form of a prayer.** ("God, today I'm thankful for...") Have them be as specific as possible. Instead of just saying they're thankful for their parents, have them come up with a specific reason they're thankful. The more specific they can get, the better.
- **Next, have them write down what they think God would say in response to the things they're grateful for.** This might be difficult at first if the kids don't know God's character very well. You may need to explain that God will always respond to us in love, and any judgmental, hurtful, or negative thoughts that come to their minds is not from God.

GOD SAVED YOU AND ME!

- **After the Interactive Gratitude is complete, have the kids take several deep breaths.** This will help calm their minds and bodies so they can better participate in the next portion.
- **Once everyone appears calm and relaxed, have them write down some things they want to pray about.** Have them write these things down as though God were sitting next to them having a conversation with them. ("God, the bully at school is really bothering me.") To begin, it might be best to keep things simple. Have them pray for things on their radar: bullies at school, a subject in school they're struggling with, their parent's jobs, their siblings. At this point, we don't want them to go too deep until they really start understanding how to hear God's voice.
- If they have trouble coming up with subjects, give them some ideas such as praying they sleep well at night, or get up on time, or if they're willing they can pray for God to give them a desire to get to know Him. As long as the prayer is true for them they can pray about it. We don't want them to pray just to go through the motions.
- **Once they have one or two items, have them write as though God were responding to them. Begin with how God sees them.** For example, "I see you sitting in your classroom wondering what to pray about. I see how concerned you are about this issue. I see how worried you are about this."
- **Once they've written a sentence or two on that, move to "I hear you".** For example, "I hear you crying at night about this issue. I hear you telling me you want me to fix this. I hear you telling your parents how worried you are about the bully at school."
- **Next, have them write a couple sentences that start with "I understand how hard this is for you."** For example, "I understand how hard it is for you to go to school every day knowing there is a bully there, waiting." There may be some things the kids pray about that this wouldn't apply to. If that is the case, they can skip this step.
- **Next, they'll write a couple sentences starting with "I'm glad to be with you."** For example, "I'm glad to be with you as you tell me about this issue. I'm glad to be with you when you're crying at night. I'm glad to be with you even when you struggle with negative emotions."
- **The last writing prompt to give them is, "I can do something about what you're going through."** This one might be harder if the kids don't understand God's character. In this case, God might respond by giving us a Bible verse reminding us of His goodness, His love, His faithfulness, etc. or He might remind us of a time in our past when we got through another difficult situation. Here is an example of what He might say, "I will help you continue to see more clearly who I am and what I've been doing in your life. When you feel scared, remember I'm with you." Remind the kids God will only say things that are loving, kind, and compassionate.
- **Finally, if anyone wants to share what God said to them, allow them some time for this.** This is an important step, and if you are able to spend time during the week before class practicing this method, it will help the kids be more comfortable with sharing if you are able to share from your own notebook.

Angela E. Powell

GOD SAVED YOU AND ME AT HOME!

LESSON SUMMARY: Today we learned about temptation. We looked at the story of when Jesus prayed in the garden before He was arrested. He told His disciples to pray so they would be able to resist temptation. We then looked to see what happened when they didn't do what Jesus asked.

MEMORY VERSE: Romans 8:11 – The Spirit of God, who raised Jesus from the dead, lives in you. And just as God raised Jesus Christ from the dead, He will give life to your mortal bodies by this same Spirit living within you.

IN THE CAR
- Discuss things that tempt each person in your home. Maybe its food, chocolate, video games, sleeping, or other things. Talk about why these are so tempting for you.
- Ask each person in your home if they've ever tried praying when they've been tempted. If so, have them tell you how it helped them. If not, challenge each other to try it out this week.
- Discuss times when you've been tempted at work and school. What can we do when we're feeling temped?

AT MEALTIMES
- Read the verses from our lesson today **(Luke 23:39-53)** then talk about ways in which Jesus might have been tempted.
- Pray as a family before your meal. Ask God to help each of you with a temptation you're facing.
- Hard boil an egg and have it with you during your meals. Remind each other how the egg helps us to know what to pray for, then spend time praying for those things as a family. **(Shell = Protection. Pray for those who protect us. Egg White = Things that surround you. Pray for parents, friends, family, pets, etc. Yoke = You. Talk to God about you. Your hopes and dreams, needs, your day, emotions you felt, etc.)**

AT BEDTIME
- Practice your memory verse.
- Spend time praying and asking God to help you overcome temptation. Be specific if you can.
- Talk about temptations you faced during the day and how you can avoid or overcome them in the future.

PRAYER REQUESTS:

God And Me

GOD SAVED YOU AND ME!

SUPPLIES NEEDED

Copies of take home sheet on page 104	Raw egg	Plastic container
Blindfolds Prayer Notebooks	Masking tape	Bean bags
Game cones	Random objects for obstacles	

LESSON 4: GOOD FRIDAY – JESUS DIES

WELCOME

As you welcome children to class, have this question written on a white board, piece of paper, or ask the question to each child as you welcome them. Have the children find someone they don't know very well and discuss it.

Ice Breaker Question: What is something you will NEVER do again?

GAME

TRUST ME

SUPPLIES: Blindfolds, Masking tape, Game cones, Bean bags, Other random objects for obstacles

- Before class, create a path using masking tape.
- Divide kids into groups of two.
- Blindfold one child in each group and have the children line up at one end of the path.
- If you have older kids, you can add obstacles in the path to make the game more challenging.
- When you say go, the child who is not blindfolded will direct the blindfolded child through the path using only verbal cues.
- When all the kids have made it through, have the kids in each team switch blindfolds and play the game again.

LESSON 4: GOOD FRIDAY – JESUS DIES

ASK: How would you react if someone snuck up behind you and scared you?

Discuss how people will jump, scream, cry, run away, or even try to fight when scared. You can also find video's online of people being scared. Just make sure to preview for language and content. There is a link where you can find videos on the unit overview page for this unit or you can use your own.

ASK: Can we control how we react when someone or something scares us?

Angela E. Powell

GOD SAVED YOU AND ME!

SAY: Yes and no. If you took a lot of time and learned tools on how to change your reaction you could, but most of us don't, or won't and it's just how we react. This is called fight, flight, or freeze mode.

ASK: What happens when people get really angry?

SAY: They might yell, their face might turn red, and some people cry when they're angry. When we're only a little bit angry, it's not as hard to choose how we'll act, but when we get really angry sometimes we do things without thinking.

SAY: After Jesus was arrested, a lot of people were feeling some really big emotions. His followers were afraid. Some of them ran and hid, some tried to fight, and we saw last week that Peter pretended not to know Jesus.

HANDS-ON ACTIVITY

SUPPLIES: Raw egg, Plastic container

- Break an egg into a container, shell and all.
- Hand it to a child and ask them to put the egg back together.

SAY: When we have really big emotions, sometimes we do things without thinking, and those things we do or say have consequences. We might break something or say hurtful words. Pilate was the person who had to decide if Jesus should be punished or not. Pilate didn't think Jesus had done anything wrong and didn't want to kill Jesus. This made the people who didn't like Jesus really angry.

SAY: When we react to those big emotions in bad ways, like saying hurtful words, it's like breaking an egg. The egg can't be put back together, and the words you say can't be erased. Friends and family might not be able to trust you as much as they did before. We may not be able to control how we react when we experience a fight, flight, or freeze moment, but there are tools we can learn to help us deal with situations before our emotions get too big.

SAY: Let's read what happened when Jesus was taken to Pilate. As we read, I want you to pay attention to how people acted.

READ THE WORD

Have the kids follow along as the teacher or older kids read the following verses. **Luke 23:1-25**

ASK: How do you think Pilate was feeling?

GOD SAVED YOU AND ME!

SAY: Frustrated, scared, and pressured to do something that wasn't right. Pilate knew Jesus hadn't done anything wrong but the crowd of people scared him.

ASK: Why do you think he was afraid of the crowd?

SAY: In Matthew, it says the Jewish leaders convinced the crowd to have Jesus killed. They spread their anger to other people. When a large group of people get angry, they can be dangerous. Pilate knew if the people got even angrier, no one would be able to calm them down, so that's why he gave in and let them kill Jesus. And some of the people in the crowd were people who'd had a party for Jesus just a week earlier! Pilate couldn't take it back just like the egg can't be fixed. Pilate didn't know how to calm the people down without giving into their demands. He didn't have the right tools.

ASK: How did Jesus act through all of this? Do we see Him yelling at people?

SAY: Remember last week, we read about Jesus praying in the garden for strength? Right after that He was arrested. He was in a lot of pain because He'd been beaten and He might have cried because of that but He wasn't angry. He didn't try to run away or fight. In fact, Jesus doesn't say very much at all. Let's read what Jesus said after they put Him on the cross.

READ THE WORD: Have the kids follow along as the teacher or older kids read the following verses. **Luke 23:34-38**

SAY: Jesus wasn't angry. He made sure his mother, Mary, would be taken care of. He was able to think of others even while going through a very scary and unfair situation. He forgave all the people for what they were doing while they were angry. See, all of these people were breaking eggs with their big emotions. They were so angry they were letting someone die who hadn't done anything wrong. They weren't going to be able to fix that.

ASK: When those people calmed down and realized what they'd done, how do you think they felt?

SAY: Probably guilty, or sad. But God had a plan.

ASK: Who created the egg?

SAY: God did.

ASK: Do you think God could put this egg back together if He wanted to?

GOD SAVED YOU AND ME!

SAY: I bet He could.

ASK: What do we do when we hurt someone's feelings or get caught doing something we shouldn't? We apologize, right?

SAY: We can't put the egg back together but we can apologize and try to do the right thing in the future. We can clean up our mess. That's how we learn. We make mistakes and we try to learn from them. But God wanted to do much more than that. When Jesus was on the cross He forgave the people for breaking so many eggs while they were angry.

ASK: Do you know what happens when God forgives us?

SAY: He makes the egg whole again. God wouldn't be able to make the egg whole again unless Jesus had died on the cross and rose again. Every mistake we make, every sin we commit, is a broken egg. We can't put the egg back together again, but God can. Our relationship with God can never be hurt. We can't lose God's trust, and He won't stop loving us if we keep doing wrong things.

ASK: Do you know why?

SAY: Because He wants to have a relationship with you. He wants you to know you can go to Him with any problem. You can go to Him with a whole carton of broken eggs and He will still welcome you with a smile. When we go to God with all our mistakes and let Him heal us, then He can start to teach us. God will teach us how to react in good ways when we have big emotions.

SAY: Here are some tools we can use to help us get through hard situations without blowing up.

Deep Breathing
SAY: Taking deep breaths can help us calm down when we start feeling big emotions rising in us. Let's practice a few times. Place a hand on your belly. Breath in through your nose until your belly sticks out. Now breathe out, slowly, through your mouth.

ASK: Can anyone tell a difference in their body? Do you feel calmer?

GOD SAVED YOU AND ME!

Appreciation

SAY: The next tool we can use is appreciation, or being thankful. When you feel big emotions rising, start thinking of things you're thankful for. If you struggle, ask God to bring things to your mind. You can also do the Interactive Gratitude we do during prayer circles sometimes.

SAY: This week I want you to practice talking to God about all of your emotions.

MEMORY VERSE

SAY: Let's say our memory verse a few times.

Romans 8:11 – The Spirit of God, who raised Jesus from the dead, lives in you. And just as God raised Jesus Christ from the dead, He will give life to your mortal bodies by this same Spirit living within you.

PRAYER CIRCLES - Groups

As the children are learning to pray and hear God's voice, it can be helpful to give them each a notebook where they can write down what they're hearing and keep track of what they've been praying for. Keep these notebooks in class until you finish this curriculum. Encourage the kids to write down prayer requests they, or their peers have on the take home sheet so they can be reminded to pray for those things during the week.

- Have kids get into groups of three or four with at least one older child or leader in each group.
- Have the kids share their prayer requests with the others in their group.
- Encourage each child to pray for one of the prayer requests presented.
- If no one has prayer requests or there aren't enough for everyone to pray about, give them suggestions such as, praying for a good, safe week for everyone or God would bring in more kids.
- If some groups finish before others, encourage the children to write down the prayer requests they heard in their group and/or spend time trying to hear God's voice.

Angela E. Powell

GOD SAVED YOU AND ME AT HOME!

LESSON SUMMARY: Today we looked at big emotions people felt from the time Jesus was arrested to His death. We learned when we have big emotions sometimes we break things or hurt people. Like an egg that's been cracked open, the trust we had is broken and is very hard to put back together. We also learned some tools we can use to help us when our emotions start feeling big. We also looked at Jesus' response in these stressful and painful moments and how He responds to us when we have big emotions. Jesus will never draw away and He can heal relationships if we'll let Him.

MEMORY VERSE: Romans 8:11 – The Spirit of God, who raised Jesus from the dead, lives in you. And just as God raised Jesus Christ from the dead, He will give life to your mortal bodies by this same Spirit living within you.

IN THE CAR
- Discuss times when each person in your family has experienced big emotions. If it's possible, without bringing the big emotions back, talk about what caused those big emotions.
- When talking about big emotions, sometimes those emotions can resurface. Practice taking deep breaths when those big emotions rise. Find ways to remind each person in your family to do this too.
- Everyone needs different things to help them calm down after feeling big emotions. Some need to be alone, while others need to talk it out. Talk about each family member's needs.

AT MEALTIMES
- Practice your memory verse.
- Take turns discussing any big emotions each person may have felt throughout the day. Have everyone take deep breaths and/or think of a memory that makes you smile between turns.
- Read through the story of Jesus being arrested and dying with your family. Talk about how Jesus acted through it all. **Luke 23:1-25, 34-38**.

AT BEDTIME
- In class we thought of things we're thankful for. Grow your thankful list each night.
- Pray and ask God to remind you to take deep breaths or think of happy memories to help you when your family isn't around to help.
- Practice deep breathing to help you relax before bedtime.

PRAYER REQUESTS:

GOD SAVED YOU AND ME!

> **SUPPLIES NEEDED**
>
> Copies of take home sheet on page 112
> Bible history videos (optional)
> Worksheet from page 106
> Prayer Notebooks
> Rotten egg
> Clear cup with water
> Info about your church
> Fresh egg
> 2 Containers
> Pens or pencils

LESSON 5: RESURRECTION SUNDAY – JESUS IS ALIVE!

NOTE: This lesson needs a rotten egg in the shell. To do this, leave an egg in a warm place for several days. Make sure one container you use for this lesson can be thrown away after using.

WELCOME

As you welcome children to class, have this question written on a white board, piece of paper, or ask the question to each child as you welcome them. Have the children find someone they don't know very well and discuss it.

Ice Breaker Question: What do you spend the most time thinking about?

GAME
FACT OR FICTION

> **SUPPLIES:** Worksheet from page 106, Information about your church, Pens or pencils

- This game will require a little bit of preparation. Print out the worksheet on page 106 to help you.
- Fill out the questions and answers on the worksheet before class. The worksheet will take you around your church to investigate signs, pamphlets, cards, books, etc. Most questions will allow you to choose which items on the list will be fact and which will be fiction.
- If you can, bring a copy of the items into the classroom or, send the kids out in teams to investigate certain areas in the church.
- At the start of the game, explain that they're going to decide if something is fact or fiction. Explain the difference between the two words then read the examples at the top of the worksheet. Tell them if they aren't sure, they'll have to investigate to find out.
- If you have a lot of kids, you can copy the worksheet **(minus the answers)**, divide them into teams, and have the teams compete to see who can get the most correct answers.

Angela E. Powell

GOD SAVED YOU AND ME!

FACT OR FICTION WORKSHEET
SAMPLE QUESTIONS:

Looking at technology for too long can harm your eyesight.	Fact
A snake can unhinge its jaw to allow it to swallow its food whole.	Fact
It's impossible to remove permanent marker from a white board.	Fiction

CHURCH INFORMATION QUESTIONS:

1. The name of our church has a "The" in it.   _____

2. Our service times are _____.   _____

3. Visitors can learn about us by _____.   _____

4. Our Mission statement says _____.   _____

5. Our Pastors name is _____.   _____

6. Our Statement of Faith says _____.   _____

7. First time visitors receive _____.   _____

8. There is a sign in the _____ that says _____.   _____

9. There are #_____ rooms in the church.   _____

10. The church website is _____.   _____

11. The office phone number is _____.   _____

12. We have a ministry called _____.   _____

13. Our church has a midweek service.   _____

14. Our church has small groups that meet once a week.   _____

15. The carpet in the _____ is a _____ color.   _____

© 2019 Angela E. Powell

God And Me

GOD SAVED YOU AND ME!

LESSON 5: RESURRECTION SUNDAY – JESUS IS ALIVE!

NOTE: You will need a rotten egg for this lesson.

ASK: Do you believe fairies really exist? What about Superheroes? Unicorns? Do you believe dinosaurs existed a long time ago? Why do you believe some of these things are real, but not others?

SAY: We have proof dinosaurs were on the earth. We keep finding their bones and we can see their skeletons in museums. I have two eggs here. One egg is starting to go bad and rot, but the other is fresh.

ASK: Can you tell which is which by looking at them? What if I told you we could find out by sticking the eggs in water?

SAY: The one that floats is the bad egg and the one that sinks is the good egg.

ASK: Do you believe I'm telling you the truth? If you believe me, then I don't have to show you how it works, right?

SAY: If you trust me to tell you the truth, then it might be easy for you to believe me without me having to prove anything. But even though you have the information in your brain now, you won't really believe it unless I show you. And I will show you, but first, I want to look at our Bible story.

ASK: How many of you believe Jesus was a real person who lived on the earth a couple thousand years ago? Do you really believe it or do you just know the information because you've heard your parents and Sunday school teachers talk about it?

SAY: Let's read about Jesus being buried after He died on the cross.

READ THE WORD

Have the kids follow along as the teacher or older kids read the following verses. **Luke 23:50-56**

SAY: The Bible tells us Jesus died, just like every other human does, and His body was put in a tomb and a really big rock was rolled in front of the opening. The women who followed Jesus were going to rub Jesus' body with special spices. Those spices would have smelled really good, but they didn't get to the tomb in time and they had to wait three days before they could rub the spices on His body.

ASK: What happens when something dies or starts to go bad?

SAY: It stinks!

GOD SAVED YOU AND ME!

ASK: So when the women returned to the tomb, what do you think they were expecting?

SAY: They believed Jesus was dead. Even though Jesus told them He would die and be raised from the dead, they only believed He had died. They knew what Jesus had said, but they didn't believe it. So they were expecting to see a smelly, dead body. Let's read what happened.

READ THE WORD
Have the kids follow along as the teacher or older kids read the following verses. **Luke 24:1-12**

ASK: The Bible says two angels appeared to the women. Do you believe angels are real? Have any of you seen an angel before? For those of you who haven't, how do you know angels are real?

SAY: The women believed in angels, and they believed what the angels told them so they ran to tell Jesus' followers. But only two of His followers ran to see the empty tomb for themselves. The others didn't believe at all. Even after Peter saw the empty tomb he wasn't sure if he believed Jesus really did come back to life. It says, "He walked away wondering what had happened." It wasn't until Jesus Himself showed up, alive and well, that the disciples believed. Let's read about that.

READ THE WORD
Have the kids follow along as the teacher or older kids read the following verses. **Luke 24:35-43**

SAY: There is a difference between knowing something and believing something. Sometimes we might think we believe something because we've heard it so many times. Earlier I told you a rotten egg would float and a fresh egg would sink. You all know that now, but let's see if I can make you believe it.

HANDS-ON ACTIVITY
SUPPLIES: Two see through containers, Water, One fresh egg, One rotten egg
- Put both eggs into the water.
- Once the kids see that one of the eggs is floating, take it out and break it open into a container.
- Let the kids smell it.

ASK: Pretty smelly right? Now do you believe a rotten egg will float and a fresh egg will sink?

SAY: Just to be sure, let's open the other egg. **(Crack the second egg into the second container)** This egg would make a great omelet.

God And Me

GOD SAVED YOU AND ME!

SAY: Jesus' followers didn't believe Jesus came back from the dead until He appeared to them and showed them He wasn't a ghost by eating some food. But once they realized Jesus really had died and come back to life, it changed their lives forever. They told everyone about Jesus. They told people about His teachings, about how He was born and how He died and came back to life to save us from sin.

ASK: But all this happened more than two thousand years ago, so how can we get proof today? The Bible tells us Jesus is still alive today, so we should be able to talk to Him right?

SAY: If you like doing research, or if you like science, you could look for books from people who have studied things like archeology, or history, and see what they've found. We also have the Bible that is like a history book to tell us all about God.

SAY: It's important to know if you really believe something or if you just know about it. The disciples knew Jesus, but they didn't fully believe in him. The things we fully believe in can change our lives in exciting ways.

NOTE: If there is extra time, you can watch Bible history videos online. There is a link where you can find videos on the unit overview page for this unit or you can use your own. Invite kids to ask you questions, or pray for salvation after the lesson, or after class. Be sure to tell the parents if their children make a decision to accept Jesus.

MEMORY VERSE
SAY: Let's say our memory verse a few times.

Romans 8:11 – The Spirit of God, who raised Jesus from the dead, lives in you. And just as God raised Jesus Christ from the dead, He will give life to your mortal bodies by this same Spirit living within you.

PRAYER CIRCLES - "God With Me" Prayer
As the children learn to pray and hear God's voice, it can be helpful to give them each a notebook so they can keep track of what they hear and are praying for. Keep these notebooks in a safe place in class until you finish this curriculum. Encourage the kids to write down prayer requests they, or their peers have, on the take home sheet so they can be reminded to pray for those things during the week. For more information on this method of prayer, please look in the reference section on page 207.
- Hand each child a notebook they'll be able to use in class for the duration of this curriculum, and a pen or pencil. Tell the kids not to write in their notebooks until they are ready to write what they're hearing from the Lord.

GOD SAVED YOU AND ME!

- **Begin with Interactive Gratitude. Have the kids think of two or three things they're grateful for.** At first, they can start with things, but try to encourage them to list what they appreciate about their peers, teachers, parents, and other people they encounter every day.
- **Have the kids write down what they're thankful for in the form of a prayer.** ("God, today I'm thankful for…") Have them be as specific as possible. Instead of just saying they're thankful for their parents, have them come up with a specific reason they're thankful. The more specific they can get, the better.
- **Next, have them write down what they think God would say in response to the things they're grateful for.** This might be difficult at first if the kids don't know God's character very well. You may need to explain that God will always respond to us in love, and any judgmental, hurtful, or negative thoughts that come to their minds is not from God.
- **After the Interactive Gratitude is complete, have the kids take several deep breaths.** This will help calm their minds and bodies so they can better participate in the next portion.
- **Once everyone appears calm and relaxed, have them write down some things they want to pray about.** Have them write these things down as though God were sitting next to them having a conversation with them. ("God, the bully at school is really bothering me.") To begin, it might be best to keep things simple. Have them pray for things on their radar: bullies at school, a subject in school they're struggling with, their parents jobs, their siblings. At this point, we don't want them to go too deep until they really start understanding how to hear God's voice.
- If they have trouble coming up with subjects, give them some ideas such as praying they sleep well at night, or get up on time, or if they're willing they can pray for God to give them a desire to get to know Him. As long as the prayer is true for them they can pray about it. We don't want them to pray just to go through the motions.
- **Once they have one or two items, have them write as though God were responding to them. Begin with how God sees them.** For example, "I see you sitting in your classroom wondering what to pray about. I see how concerned you are about this issue. I see how worried you are about this."
- **Once they've written a sentence or two on that, move to "I hear you".** For example, "I hear you crying at night about this issue. I hear you telling me you want me to fix this. I hear you telling your parents how worried you are about the bully at school."
- **Next, have them write a couple sentences that start with "I understand how hard this is for you."** For example, "I understand how hard it is for you to go to school every day knowing there is a bully there, waiting." There may be some things the kids pray about that this wouldn't apply to. If that is the case, they can skip this step.

GOD SAVED YOU AND ME!

- **Next, have them write a couple of sentences that start with "I'm glad to be with you."** For example, "I'm glad to be with you right now as you tell me about this issue. I'm glad to be with you when you're crying in your bed at night. I'm glad to be with you even when you're struggling with negative emotions."
- **The last writing prompt to give them is, "I can do something about what you're going through."** This one might be harder if the kids don't understand God's character. In this case, God might respond by giving us a Bible verse reminding us of His goodness, His love, His faithfulness, etc. or He might remind us of a time in our past when we got through another difficult situation. Here is an example of what He might say, "I will help you continue to see more clearly who I am and what I've been doing in your life. I am protecting you. When you're feeling scared, remember I'm with you." Remind the kids that God will only say things that are loving, kind, and compassionate.
- **Finally, if anyone wants to share what God said to them, allow them some time for this.** This is an important step, and if you are able to spend time during the week before class practicing this method, it will help the kids be more comfortable with sharing if you are able to share from your own notebook.

Angela E. Powell

GOD SAVED YOU AND ME AT HOME!

LESSON SUMMARY: In this lesson we looked at the difference between knowing something and believing something. Before Jesus' death, He told His followers, several times, He would die and be raised from the dead three days later. They knew this, but it's clear by their actions they didn't believe it. Kids raised in church are told Bible stories so often, they know them by heart, but at some point they have to choose to believe the Bible is true for themselves. This lesson gives the children tools on how they can make that decision.

MEMORY VERSE: Romans 8:11 – The Spirit of God, who raised Jesus from the dead, lives in you. And just as God raised Jesus Christ from the dead, He will give life to your mortal bodies by this same Spirit living within you.

IN THE CAR
- Pick a story from the Bible and talk about why you believe it's true, or why you struggle to believe it's true.
- Discuss things you've heard at school. Are they things you know about or things you believe? Why do we believe them?
- Talk about things that would amaze you if you found out they were actually true or real.

AT MEALTIMES
- Get online with your parents and look for books and videos that prove the Bible is true. At mealtimes, read a small part of the book and talk about it.
- Read through the verses from class again. Talk about how different people reacted to the news of Jesus being raised from the dead. **Luke 24:1-2; 35-43**.
- Play your own game of "Fact or Fiction". Have each person say one thing that may or may not be true and have everyone guess if it's fact or fiction.

AT BEDTIME
- Practice hearing God's voice each night. Remember He talks to us through our thoughts, our emotions, and by putting images in our minds. Everything He says to us has to line up with what the Bible says. Start simple. Ask Him how He feels about you. Ask Him to remind you of a happy memory.

PRAYER REQUESTS:

God And Me

UNIT 4

UNIT THEME: GOD MAKES YOU AND ME MIGHTY

This unit looks at some of the heroes in the Bible and shows us that being a hero is much more than having a cool costume and being really strong. We'll look at Esther and Gideon to see how God used them to save their people. Then we'll look at verses to show how God gives us strength. These lessons follow a skit format so you'll need an adult helper or volunteer to play the role of the superhero. There are also suggestions at the end of each lesson on how to adapt it for a one teacher classroom.

The superhero doesn't have a specific name. Instead, there is a list of options to choose from below. This way, you can have a superhero that fits costumes you might already have on hand, you can have a different superhero visit every week, or you can make up your own name to fit your children's ministry.

Suggested Superhero names:

| Captain Sprinkles | The Red Shadow | Spider Monkey Girl/Boy |
| Wonder Llama | Math Man/Woman | |

Lesson 1: God Gave Queen Esther Courage
In this lesson we learn what courage is and how God can help us have courage when we don't feel like we have any.

Lesson 2: Gideon The Scared Soldier
In this lesson we see how God takes a man from being afraid, to leading an army into battle. We'll also see how admitting our weaknesses to God is a good thing because God takes those weaknesses and shows everyone how powerful He is.

Lesson 3: God Renews Our Strength
This lesson looks at how God renews our strength when we're tired, or overworked and how He is able to do this. We'll also see that God never gets tired and is always available to us.

Lesson 4: God Gives Me Strength
This lesson looks at the life of Paul who learned to be content with little, and content with a lot. We'll see life is not about who has the most toys, but about trusting in and having a relationship with God. When we trust God completely we won't ever have to worry.

Lesson 5: The Armor of God
This lesson looks at the armor God has provided us and how we can use it in our lives today.

Optional Videos For This Unit: https://bit.ly/2GYt34k

Angela E. Powell

GOD MAKES YOU AND ME MIGHTY!

SUPPLIES NEEDED

Copies of take home sheet on page 120		Cups
Masking tape	Superhero cape	Water
Superhero mask	Toy rat, spider, or snake	Blindfolds
Sealable sandwich bag	Sharpened pencils	Prayer Notebooks

LESSON 1: GOD GAVE QUEEN ESTHER COURAGE.

WELCOME

As you welcome children to class, have this question written on a white board, piece of paper, or ask the question to each child as you welcome them. Have the children find someone they don't know very well and discuss it.

Ice Breaker Question: What would be your ideal way to spend the weekend?

GAME

TRUSTING GOD IN THE MINEFIELD

SUPPLIES: Cups, Blindfolds, Masking tape

- Before class, make a large square on the floor with masking tape. This will be the minefield.
- Set up cups randomly in the minefield. These are the mines.
- If you have a lot of kids, you may want to make several squares and have teams compete.
- Divide kids into pairs. The one who wears the blindfold will walk through the minefield.
- When you say "Go" the child not wearing a blindfold will attempt to direct the blindfolded child through the minefield. If the child with the blindfold runs into any of the cups, the game is over.
- Children from other teams can try to distract the children going through the minefield with talking or yelling so the blindfolded child has a harder time hearing their teammate, but they can't call out directions to make them run into cups

LESSON 1: GOD GAVE QUEEN ESTHER COURAGE

NOTE: The lessons in this unit use a superhero as an object lesson/skit. It is best if you can have someone dress up as the superhero, however if you don't have someone who can play the superhero, there are notes at the end on how you can modify this lesson.

Before class, set a toy spider, rat, or snake somewhere in the room.

God And Me

GOD MAKES YOU AND ME MIGHTY!

TEACHER: Good morning everyone! We have a special guest joining us today. Help me welcome our cities newest superhero, [NAME]!

SH: Thank you, thank you. I decided to stop by when I heard you were learning about how God makes you and me mighty! God made me mighty by giving me the ability to run through brick walls without getting hurt, making me super strong, and He made me fearless, which means I'm not afraid of anything! ***Sees toy spider, rat, or snake, screams, and jumps up on a chair.***

TEACHER: What's wrong?

SH: Spider (rat/snake)! I hate spiders (rats/snakes)!

TEACHER: *picks up toy* It's not real, it's just a toy. I thought you said God made you fearless?

SH: He did, but spiders (rats/snakes) are just icky. ***Shudders***

TEACHER: Kids, do you really think God makes us mighty by letting us run through walls, or giving us super strength?

TEACHER: No, God makes us mighty in different ways. Why don't you stay for our lesson and see how God helped a young woman in the Bible be mighty.

SH: Okay, but only if there are no spiders (rats/snakes) in the story.

TEACHER: No spiders (rats/snakes). This story is about a young woman who became a Queen. Her name was Esther. She was very brave because of a promise God gave to her people. Esther has a whole book in the Bible that tells her story. We aren't going to read the whole thing, but we are going to look at some sections of the book.

TEACHER: Xerxes was the King of Persia. Many Jewish people lived in Persia because they'd lost their country, Israel, in war. The king was married to a woman named Vashti, but she made the king angry and he banished her.

ASK: Does anyone know what "banished" means?

Angela E. Powell

GOD MAKES YOU AND ME MIGHTY!

TEACHER: It means the king sent her away and told her she could never come back.

After a while, the king decided he wanted to marry again. So all the unmarried young women were gathered together and for one whole year they had special training and spa treatments. Let's read about that.

READ THE WORD
Have the kids follow along as the teacher or older kids read the following verses. **Esther 2:8-12, 15-20**

TEACHER: Why do you think Esther's cousin, Mordecai, told her not to tell anyone she was a Jew?

TEACHER: The Bible doesn't really give us an answer to that question but we can see Esther trusted Mordecai because she obeys his instructions. It could be that Mordecai knew the Jews weren't liked very well. Sometime after Esther became queen, the king hired a man named Haman to be in charge of everyone in the palace.

SH: Let me guess, Haman is the bad guy?

TEACHER: He sure is, and Haman had more power than anyone except the king. The king also commanded everyone to bow to Haman whenever he walked by them. Mordecai refused to bow to Haman because God had commanded the Jews not to bow to anyone but God. This made Haman so mad he decided to use his power in a bad way. Let's read what Haman did.

READ THE WORD
Have the kids follow along as the teacher or older kids read the following verses. **Esther 3:8-11**

TEACHER: Instead of punishing Mordecai for not bowing to him, Haman decided ALL the Jews should die, and he tricked the king into agreeing to this. Mordecai heard about Haman's plan and was really upset. He told Esther what was happening and asked her to go to the king to beg for their lives. Let's read Esther's response.

READ THE WORD
Have the kids follow along as the teacher or older kids read the following verses. **Esther 4:11-16**

TEACHER: Why do you think Esther wanted them to pray before she went to see the king?

SH: She wanted God to give her super powers so she could beat up Haman!

GOD MAKES YOU AND ME MIGHTY!

TEACHER: Not quite. Esther knew if she went to the king without being called, the king could have her killed, so Esther needed God to give her courage and favor with the king. All the Jewish people knew God had set them apart to be His special people. It was a promise God made to them. Esther was asking God to make her mighty and give her courage.

SH: Courage is a good thing for every mighty person to have.

TEACHER: Yes it is. And after three days of praying, Esther went to the king. What do you think the king did?

SH: I hope the king didn't kill her. That would be a very sad story.

TEACHER: The king held out his golden scepter and welcomed her! Their prayers had worked!

SH: Woohoo! I knew it!

TEACHER: Esther invited the king and Haman to a dinner party. At the dinner party, the king asked her what she wanted, but Esther wasn't quite ready to tell him yet, so she invited them to another dinner party and promised to tell the king what she wanted on the second night. Let's read what happened.

READ THE WORD
Have the kids follow along as the teacher or older kids read the following verses. **Esther 7:1-8**

TEACHER: Do you think Esther was afraid, knowing she could die if the king got angry with her?

SH: I would be. I mean… of course not, I'm not afraid of anything!

TEACHER: She probably was, but she had three choices. She could risk going to the king, she could stay quiet and watch her friends and family be killed, or she could say she was a Jew and be killed with the rest of her people.

SH: None of those are very good choices.

TEACHER: Whatever Esther decided to do, she would need courage. God made her mighty by giving her the courage to do the right thing, even though it meant she might die.

Angela E. Powell

GOD MAKES YOU AND ME MIGHTY!

TEACHER: Sometimes it can be hard to do the right thing. Maybe you saw your friend cheating on a test, and were worried they wouldn't be your friend anymore if you told the teacher. Or maybe you saw someone being bullied but were afraid to tell anyone because you didn't want to be bullied. Maybe you broke or lost something that belonged to someone else. We all need courage to do the right thing.

ASK: What did Esther ask all the Jewish people to do when she needed courage?

TEACHER: She asked them to pray. When you and I are feeling scared, or like we don't have the courage or strength to do the right thing, we can pray and ask God to give us courage and make us mighty.

ASK: Would you guys like to do a fun activity that might take a little bit of courage?

HANDS-ON ACTIVITY

SUPPLIES: Sealable sandwich bags, Water, Sharpened pencils

- Fill a sandwich bag with water, leaving a little space at the top, and seal the bag closed.
- Ask the kids what would happen if we were to poke a pencil in the plastic bag.
- **SAY:** This pencil is like things we're afraid of. The water is the strength we have inside us.
- Poke the pencil straight through the bag, leaving the pencil in the bag. It shouldn't leak.
- **SAY:** We might be worried that the pencil, what we're afraid of, will make our strength leak out of us, but we can pray and ask God to give us courage, so our strength won't leak out.
- Have the kids think of something that worries them before they stick a pencil through the bag.
- You may need to have more than one bag of water depending on how many children you have.

ADAPTING THE LESSON FOR A ONE TEACHER CLASSROOM

If you only have one teacher available for this lesson, you can start by revealing to the kids you've recently become a super hero, tell them about your new found super powers, and be scared by the fake toy rat. After that, you can take your costume off, explain that maybe you are afraid of some things, and share how you've been reading about Esther to help you with courage. You would then proceed through the lesson and skip over the superhero comments.

MEMORY VERSE

SAY: Let's say our memory verse a few times.

Philippians 4:13 - For I can do everything through Christ, who gives me strength.

GOD MAKES YOU AND ME MIGHTY!

PRAYER CIRCLES - Groups

As the children are learning to pray and hear God's voice, it can be helpful to give them each a notebook where they can write down what they're hearing and keep track of what they've been praying for. Keep these notebooks in class until you finish this curriculum. Encourage the kids to write down prayer requests they, or their peers have on the take home sheet so they can be reminded to pray for those things during the week.

- Have kids get into groups of three or four with at least one older child or leader in each group.
- Have the kids share their prayer requests with the others in their group.
- Encourage each child to pray for one of the prayer requests presented.
- If no one has prayer requests or there aren't enough for everyone to pray about, give them suggestions such as, praying for a good, safe week for everyone or God would bring in more kids.
- If some groups finish before others, encourage the children to write down the prayer requests they heard in their group and/or spend time trying to hear God's voice.

Angela E. Powell

GOD MAKES YOU AND ME MIGHTY AT HOME!

LESSON SUMMARY: This lesson looks at the story of Queen Esther. We looked at why Esther had good reasons to be afraid, but she asked her people to pray for her, and she prayed too. As a result God gave her the courage to do what she needed to do in order to save her people.

MEMORY VERSE: Philippians 4:13 - For I can do everything through Christ, who gives me strength.

IN THE CAR
- Talk about courage. What does it look like today? How is it different from when Esther was queen? How is it the same?
- Ask your parents what kinds of things they needed courage for when they were your age. Do you need courage for the same things or different things?
- Talk about why the adults in your life need courage. Make a plan to pray that God would give each member of your family courage to do the right things.

AT MEALTIMES
- Our world is very different today than it was when Esther was alive, but people who follow God still need courage. Talk about ways Christians today need courage.
- Courage isn't just about being brave. Talk about what else courage could be.
- Talk about the superhero you met in class today. Why did they feel the need to pretend they had more courage than they really did? Are there times when you have felt like you had to act a certain way, but it wasn't really you? Discuss those times with your family.

AT BEDTIME
- Pray for God to give you courage to do what He wants you to do.
- Ask God what you can do for Him this week, then pray for the courage to do it.
- Ask your parents to pray for you the way the Jewish people prayed for Esther.

PRAYER REQUESTS:

God And Me

GOD MAKES YOU AND ME MIGHTY!

SUPPLIES NEEDED

Copies of take home sheet on page 129	Superhero cape	Superhero mask
Glass jar	Index card	Water
Images or video examples of Ram's Horn, Clay Jars, and Torches		Prayer Notebooks

LESSON 2: GIDEON THE SCARED SOLDIER

WELCOME

As you welcome children to class, have this question written on a white board, piece of paper, or ask the question to each child as you welcome them. Have the children find someone they don't know very well and discuss it.

Ice Breaker Question: What is your favorite T.V. show?

GAME

HEEL-TO-TOE

SUPPLIES: None

- Before class, decide how far the kids will have to walk/run for this game. The longer the better.
- Divide the kids into teams of about five.
- The goal of each team is to get everyone across the finish line, but they have to walk heel-to-toe. All the kids will start walking heel-to-toe when you say, "Go".
- Designate one person from each team to be the "Helper". If the helper holds hands with one of their teammates, they can walk or run to the finish line, but the helper can only help one teammate at a time.
- The Helper can only run when they are holding hands with a teammate. If they are walking back to help another teammate, they have to walk heel-to-toe.
- Use this game as an object lesson: God makes us mighty when we stay connected to Him.

LESSON 2: GIDEON THE SCARED SOLDIER

NOTE: The lessons in this unit use a superhero as an object lesson/skit. It is best if you can have someone dress up as the superhero, however if you don't have someone who can play the superhero, there are notes at the end on how you can modify this lesson.

NOTE: This lesson will work with the same superhero as last week, or a different one.

Angela E. Powell

GOD MAKES YOU AND ME MIGHTY!

TEACHER: We have a special guest with us again today! Welcome [NAME]! They're going to tell you all about their cool gadgets today!

SH: Who told you I have cool gadgets? Who have you been talking to?

TEACHER: No one, but don't all superheroes have cool gadgets to help them catch the bad guys?

SH: Oh, yes, of course. But they're top secret, I can't tell you about them or show them to you. How do I know these kids aren't working for my enemy, Dark Thunder?

TEACHER: You know, it seems like you're afraid to trust us.

SH: What? I'm a superhero, I'm not afraid of anything.

TEACHER: Sometimes we need to admit to God when we are weak so He can help us be strong.

SH: What weakness? I don't have any weaknesses. What have you heard?

TEACHER: I haven't heard anything, but we're all human, which means we all have areas in our lives where we are weak and other areas where we are strong. If we take the weak areas to God, He can help us.

SH: I don't need any help. I'm a superhero. I can do superhero things all by myself.

TEACHER: I'm sure you can. Would you like to stay and listen to our lesson today? It's about a man who was afraid of everything, but God used this man to win a war.

SH: Sounds interesting, but I'm not sitting by that kid *point to random kid*. They look like they want to touch my cape and I don't like having my cape touched. *Sits next to a different child*. Don't touch my cape.

TEACHER: Our lesson today is about a man named Gideon. After God rescued the Israelites from slavery in Egypt, He gave them their own country. But God gave them rules to follow in this new country, just like we have rules in our classroom, or at home.

GOD MAKES YOU AND ME MIGHTY!

TEACHER: For a while, the Israelites obeyed these rules, but eventually they started to disobey God and God had to give them a consequence, just like our parents give us consequences when we disobey them. Their consequence was that for seven years, their neighbors, the Midianites came over to Israel and destroyed all their crops, and stole all their cattle, goats, and sheep. They made it so Israel didn't have any food for seven years.

SH: That sounds like something Dark Thunder would do.

TEACHER: The Israelites tried to grow crops in secret and some of them were successful, but it wasn't enough to keep everyone fed. Finally the Israelites prayed to God and asked Him to rescue them. They said they were sorry for disobeying God and promised they would follow the rules again. So God sent an angel to Gideon. Let's read what happened.

READ THE WORD
Have the kids follow along as the teacher or older kids read the following verses. **Judges 6:12-17**

TEACHER: The angel told Gideon he was a mighty hero, but did Gideon act like a mighty hero?

SH: No, a real hero wouldn't be hiding from the enemy!

TEACHER: God made Gideon to be mighty, but Gideon didn't believe that. He believed he was the weakest person in all of Israel. But what does God tell him?

TEACHER: God told Gideon it didn't matter if he was the weakest person in his family because God would be with Gideon, and God had enough strength to help Gideon. But Gideon didn't trust the angel. He wanted God to give him a sign.

SH: Gideon sounds like a superhero who doesn't know he's a superhero.

TEACHER: That's exactly right, [NAME]. But God wanted to show Gideon he really was mighty, so Gideon cooked a meal and brought it to the angel. The angel touched the food and fire came out of the rock it was sitting on and burned up the food! Finally Gideon believed the angel had been sent by God, but he still didn't believe God could make him mighty. Let's read what happened when the Midianites came back to destroy Israel's food again.

READ THE WORD
Have the kids follow along as the teacher or older kids read the following verses. **Judges 6:33-37a.**

Angela E. Powell

GOD MAKES YOU AND ME MIGHTY!

TEACHER: Here it says God gave Gideon extra strength, but Gideon was still afraid and wanted God to give him another sign. God already gave Gideon all the strength he needed, but Gideon didn't have a very close relationship with God and didn't know he could trust God. So God decided to give Gideon two more signs instead of just one.

ASK: Why do you think God gave Gideon so many signs?

SH: It's like when Superman thought he was just Clark Kent. He didn't know he was from a different planet and it took a while for him to believe it was true.

TEACHER: That's right. Gideon wanted to trust God. He'd heard stories of God rescuing the Israelites in the past, but he wasn't sure God would do it again. God was patient with Gideon. God wanted Gideon to be able to trust Him and God knew Gideon needed these signs so he could trust God would keep His promise. I'm going to show you how Gideon must have been feeling. Who here trusts me?

HANDS-ON ACTIVITY

SUPPLIES: Glass jar, Index card, Water

NOTE: You may need to practice this a few times before class.
- Hold up the jar of water and place the index card over the opening.
- **ASK:** What do you think will happen if I turn this upside down? Will the index card keep the water from coming out?
- Flip the jar upside down while holding the index card in place.
- **ASK:** Does anyone trust me enough to stand under the jar when I take my hand away?
- If you get a volunteer great, if not, you can have your superhero kneel under the jar.
- Remove your hand. The index card will keep the water from coming out of the jar.

ASK: Were you guys worried you might get wet if you stood under the jar?

TEACHER: Gideon felt the same way about trusting God, but after the two signs, Gideon believed God would rescue the Israelites. He gathered the people and got a big army together. Would you be more willing to stand under the jar now that you've seen it doesn't leak? That's why God's signs were so helpful to Gideon. Let's read what happened next.

READ THE WORD
Have the kids follow along as the teacher or older kids read the following verses. **Judges 7:2-7.**

GOD MAKES YOU AND ME MIGHTY!

TEACHER: How can we tell Gideon trusted God in this passage? Gideon was afraid at the beginning, right? Well, here, God tells Gideon that anyone who is afraid can go home. Did Gideon go home? No, he wasn't afraid anymore because he trusted God would help him.

TEACHER: After God tells Gideon to send anyone who is afraid, home, God has Gideon send even more people home and Gideon is left with only three hundred soldiers. The enemy had so many soldiers it was hard to count them all! But Gideon wasn't afraid anymore. Let's find out what happened next.

READ THE WORD
Have the kids follow along as the teacher or older kids read the following verses. **Judges 7:8b-15.**

TEACHER: Why do you think God wanted Gideon to hear that conversation?

SH: Oh, I know, He wanted Gideon to know what the enemy had planned!

TEACHER: Not exactly. It was another sign. Gideon hadn't asked for another sign, but God gave him one anyway! Now we're going to find out what cool superhero gadgets Gideon used to win the battle.

SH: Oh, I like gadgets, I can't wait! ***Looks at the child next to them*** Did you just touch my cape?

READ THE WORD
Have the kids follow along as the teacher or older kids read the following verses. **Judges 7:16-22**

TEACHER: What were Gideon's cool gadgets? A ram's horn, a clay jar, and a torch. **(Show images of each)**

SH: Those are NOT cool gadgets. Iron Man's gadgets are WAY cooler.

TEACHER: Maybe, but God wanted the Israelites to know it was God who rescued them, not Gideon, and not the cool gadgets. Gideon and his three hundred men didn't have to do much fighting. All they had to do was blow their horns, break their jars, and hold up their torches. Let's see if we can get an idea of what that sounded like. **(Play video or sound track of ram's horn and clay pots breaking. There is a link on the overview page where you can find videos for this unit or you can use your own.)**

TEACHER: God makes you and me mighty when we're willing to hear God's voice and trust Him to take care of us.

Angela E. Powell

GOD MAKES YOU AND ME MIGHTY!

SH: This Gideon sounds like a mighty hero to me. Even if he didn't believe he was a hero at first, God helped him become one. I see now that my power comes from God and I need to trust God more. But now I have to fly, there are other kids who need to hear all about my superpowers.

TEACHER: Thanks for visiting [NAME]! God didn't turn Gideon into a superhero, but He did help Gideon see he could trust God. Once Gideon was able to trust God, he was able to be God's sidekick and help save the Israelites.

TEACHER: God wants to do the same with you and me! God wants to use you in your schools, your neighborhoods, and even your families. He wants you to learn how to hear His voice and trust Him to give you strength and help you do what He wants you to do. God wants to make you and me mighty!

ADAPTING THE LESSON FOR A ONE TEACHER CLASSROOM

If you only have one teacher available for this lesson, start the lesson by reminding the kids you've recently become a super hero. Or, if there is a different teacher, explain that you've just discovered you're a superhero. You can ask the kids for advice since you're still learning about your superpowers and you aren't sure you can face your enemy, Dark Thunder, yet. Share how you've been reading about Gideon to help you with courage. Proceed through the lesson and skip over the superhero comments.

MEMORY VERSE

SAY: Let's say our memory verse a few times.

Philippians 4:13 - For I can do everything through Christ, who gives me strength.

PRAYER CIRCLES - "God With Me" Prayer

As the children learn to pray and hear God's voice, it can be helpful to give them each a notebook so they can keep track of what they hear and are praying for. Keep these notebooks in a safe place in class until you finish this curriculum. Encourage the kids to write down prayer requests they, or their peers have, on the take home sheet so they can be reminded to pray for those things during the week. For more information on this method of prayer, please look in the reference section on page 207.

- Hand each child a notebook they'll be able to use in class for the duration of this curriculum, and a pen or pencil. Tell the kids not to write in their notebooks until they are ready to write what they're hearing from the Lord.
- **Begin with Interactive Gratitude. Have the kids think of two or three things they're grateful for.** At first, they can start with things, but try to encourage them to list what they appreciate about their peers, teachers, parents, and other people they encounter every day.

GOD MAKES YOU AND ME MIGHTY!

- **Have the kids write down what they're thankful for in the form of a prayer.** ("God, today I'm thankful for…") Have them be as specific as possible. Instead of just saying they're thankful for their parents, have them come up with a specific reason they're thankful. The more specific they can get, the better.
- **Next, have them write down what they think God would say in response to the things they're grateful for.** This might be difficult at first if the kids don't know God's character very well. You may need to explain that God will always respond to us in love, and any judgmental, hurtful, or negative thoughts that come to their minds is not from God.
- **After the Interactive Gratitude is complete, have the kids take several deep breaths.** This will help calm their minds and bodies so they can better participate in the next portion.
- **Once everyone appears calm and relaxed, have them write down some things they want to pray about.** Have them write these things down as though God were sitting next to them having a conversation with them. ("God, the bully at school is really bothering me.") To begin, it might be best to keep things simple. Have them pray for things on their radar: bullies at school, a subject in school they're struggling with, their parent's jobs, their siblings. At this point, we don't want them to go too deep until they really start understanding how to hear God's voice.
- If they have trouble coming up with subjects, give them some ideas such as praying they sleep well at night, or get up on time, or if they're willing they can pray for God to give them a desire to get to know Him. As long as the prayer is true for them they can pray about it. We don't want them to pray just to go through the motions.
- **Once they have one or two items, have them write as though God were responding to them. Begin with how God sees them.** For example, "I see you sitting in your classroom wondering what to pray about. I see how concerned you are about this issue. I see how worried you are about this."
- **Once they've written a sentence or two on that, move to "I hear you".** For example, "I hear you crying at night about this issue. I hear you telling me you want me to fix this. I hear you telling your parents how worried you are about the bully at school."
- **Next, have them write a couple sentences that start with "I understand how hard this is for you."** For example, "I understand how hard it is for you to go to school every day knowing there is a bully there, waiting." There may be some things the kids pray about that this wouldn't apply to. If that is the case, they can skip this step.
- **Next, have them write a couple of sentences that start with "I'm glad to be with you."** For example, "I'm glad to be with you right now as you tell me about this issue. I'm glad to be with you when you're crying in your bed at night. I'm glad to be with you even when you're struggling with negative emotions."

GOD MAKES YOU AND ME MIGHTY!

- **The last writing prompt to give them is, "I can do something about what you're going through."** This one might be harder if the kids don't understand God's character. In this case, God might respond by giving us a Bible verse reminding us of His goodness, His love, His faithfulness, etc. or He might remind us of a time in our past when we got through another difficult situation. Here is an example of what He might say, "I will help you continue to see more clearly who I am and what I've been doing in your life. I am protecting you. When you're feeling scared, remember I'm with you." Remind the kids that God will only say things that are loving, kind, and compassionate.
- **Finally, if anyone wants to share what God said to them, allow them some time for this.** This is an important step, and if you are able to spend time during the week before class practicing this method, it will help the kids be more comfortable with sharing if you are able to share from your own notebook.

God And Me

GOD MAKES YOU AND ME MIGHTY AT HOME!

LESSON SUMMARY: Today we learned about Gideon. God gave him the strength and courage to fight the enemies of Israel, but it took some time before Gideon was able to believe it. We saw how God was patient with Gideon while Gideon learned to trust God. And we also learned that God is patient with us while we learn to trust that He has given us strength as well.

MEMORY VERSE: Philippians 4:13 - For I can do everything through Christ, who gives me strength.

IN THE CAR
- Ask your parents what they think is special about you.
- Tell each member of your family what you think is special about them.
- Have each member of your family say what they think each person's strengths are.

AT MEALTIMES
- Talk about the story of Gideon. If God asked you to do something you didn't want to do, what would it be? What would it take for you to find the courage to do that thing?
- Gideon felt like he was the least important person in his family. Talk about times you've felt like an important part of your family and times when you didn't. What makes you feel important in your family?
- The Israelites were being oppressed by the Midianites as a consequence for disobeying God, but it took a while before the Israelites were really sorry for their actions. Talk about times when you've been in trouble. How long did it take before you really felt sorry for what you said or did?

AT BEDTIME
- Ask God to tell you why He thinks you're special. Spend five minutes each night listening for God's voice. Write down what you hear and talk about it with your family.
- Encourage each person in your family to ask God to tell them why He thinks they're special and spend time listening for His voice. Talk about what He tells you.
- If you were going to ask God to give you a sign to prove you could trust Him, what would you ask Him to do? Have each person in your family answer this question.

PRAYER REQUESTS:

© 2019 Angela E. Powell

Angela E. Powell

GOD MAKES YOU AND ME MIGHTY!

SUPPLIES NEEDED

Copies of take home sheet on page 135	2 XXL long sleeved shirts	Balloons
Masking tape	Superhero cape	Superhero mask
How an eagle soars video	Prayer Notebooks	

LESSON 3: GOD RENEWS OUR STRENGTH

WELCOME

As you welcome children to class, have this question written on a white board, piece of paper, or ask the question to each child as you welcome them. Have the children find someone they don't know very well and discuss it.

Ice Breaker Question: What's your dream car?

GAME

STRONGMAN RELAY RACE

SUPPLIES: Two XXL Long sleeved shirts, Balloons, Masking tape

- Before class make two lines at least ten feet apart with the masking tape.
- Divide kids into two teams and have each team stand on one of the masking tape lines. The teams should face each other.
- Give the first person on each line, an oversized, long sleeved shirt, and place four blown up balloons on the floor next to them.
- When you say "Go" the first person on each team, will put the shirt on, stuff the balloons into the arms to make muscles, run to the other team's line, show off their muscles, and shout, "My strength comes from God!". Then they'll run back to their line, take off the shirt and balloons and the next person in line will take their turn.
- First team to finish wins.

LESSON 3: GOD RENEWS OUR STRENGTH

NOTE: The lessons in this unit use a superhero as an object lesson/skit. It is best if you can have someone dress up as the superhero, however if you don't have someone who can play the superhero, there are notes at the end on how you can modify this lesson.

NOTE: This lesson will work with the same superhero as last week, or a different one.

Superhero enters the room, tired and weak.

God And Me

GOD MAKES YOU AND ME MIGHTY!

TEACHER: What's wrong, [NAME]?

SH: I have saved our city three times this week from the evil Freeze Man, Kangaroo Boy, and Slothman. I'm exhausted. If my nemesis, Scorpion, should show his face, I don't know if I'll have the energy to defeat him.

TEACHER: Sounds like you're in need of some rest. It just so happens our lesson today is all about how God restores our strength. Would you like to join us for our lesson? Maybe you'll learn how to get your strength back with God's help!

SH: Sure, I'll stay.

TEACHER: Let's read the Bible and find out what it has to say about God's strength.

READ THE WORD

Have the kids follow along as the teacher or older kids read the following verses. **Isaiah 40:28-31.**

SH: Wait a minute. God NEVER gets weak?

TEACHER: That's right.

SH: And He can fly like an eagle?

TEACHER: Um… That's not quite what those verses said. Can anyone tell [NAME] what those verses were saying?

TEACHER: The verse says those who trust in the Lord will find new strength and they will soar high on wings like eagles.

SH: Oh, I see. So God will give all of us the ability to fly.

TEACHER: No. Isaiah is using something called a metaphor when he talks about flying like an eagle. A metaphor is a word or phrase that's applied to an object or action that isn't really true, but helps explain an idea or makes a comparison.

SH: A Meta-whosit? *Looks at child* Do you understand what the teacher said?

Angela E. Powell

GOD MAKES YOU AND ME MIGHTY!

TEACHER: Let me give you some examples of a Metaphor to help you understand. You might have heard sayings like:
- She is as sharp as a tack, which means she's really smart.
- The snow is a white blanket. It's a blanket because it covers everything.
- He is a night owl, meaning he likes to stay up late.

SH: I think I understand now, but how does soaring on eagle's wings apply to God's strength?

TEACHER: Great question! An eagle uses the wind to keep them in the air. They spread their wings really wide and soar on the wind. They don't have to flap their wings or use very much energy to fly through the air. All they have to do is use the feathers on the very end of their wings to make small adjustments in direction and speed. They can go really long distances and not get tired! Let's watch a video so you can see for yourself.

VIDEO
Show a video about how an eagle soars. There is a link on the overview page where you can find videos for this unit or you can use your own.

TEACHER: [NAME] when you're well rested and have all your strength, is it hard to fight your enemies?

SH: No, it's really easy.

TEACHER: That's how it is for the eagle.

SH: So God is like the wind the eagles soar on and when we're trusting in God, He does all the hard work and we just have to soar on His strength.

TEACHER: Yes! Exactly! God gives you and me strength when we trust Him. And since He never gets tired, He doesn't have to stop and rest like we do.

SH: God is a much better superhero than I am.

TEACHER: Yes, He's a lot stronger than all of us combined, but He's kind and loving and He's willing to share His strength with us.

SH: But how do we learn to trust God?

GOD MAKES YOU AND ME MIGHTY!

TEACHER: Great question [NAME]! Do you kids have any ideas on how we can learn to trust God?

TEACHER: Those are great suggestions! We learn to trust God when we spend time getting to know Him. We can get to know Him by learning how to pray and how to hear His voice. We can also learn about Him by reading our Bibles.

TEACHER: Just like we learn to trust our friends and family by spending time with them, we will learn to trust God when we spend time with Him.

SH: You know, just learning about how God gives us strength has made me feel stronger already. If Scorpion does show his face, I'll be able to fight him with God's help. Instead of being the superhero, I'll let God be the hero and I'll be His sidekick!

TEACHER: That's a great way to look at it! God wants to make us mighty and we can learn how by being His sidekick! Our memory verse for the month can remind us to look to God for our strength.

ADAPTING THE LESSON FOR A ONE TEACHER CLASSROOM

If you only have one teacher available for this lesson, you can start the lesson by reminding the kids you've recently become a super hero. Or, if there is a different teacher for this lesson, explaining that you've just discovered you're a superhero. You can apologize to the students for being so tired today and explain how you've been saving the city from your enemies, but you've been reading in the Bible that God gives us strength. You would then proceed through the lesson and skip over the superhero comments or use them as thoughts you've had about the verses and get feedback from the students.

MEMORY VERSE

SAY: Let's say our memory verse a few times.

Philippians 4:13 - For I can do everything through Christ, who gives me strength.

PRAYER CIRCLES - Groups

As the children are learning to pray and hear God's voice, it can be helpful to give them each a notebook where they can write down what they're hearing and keep track of what they've been praying for. Keep these notebooks in class until you finish this curriculum. Encourage the kids to write down prayer requests they, or their peers have on the take home sheet so they can be reminded to pray for those things during the week.

- Have kids get into groups of three or four with at least one older child or leader in each group.
- Have the kids share their prayer requests with the others in their group.

GOD MAKES YOU AND ME MIGHTY!

- Encourage each child to pray for one of the prayer requests presented.
- If no one has prayer requests or there aren't enough for everyone to pray about, give them suggestions such as, praying for a good, safe week for everyone or God would bring in more kids.
- If some groups finish before others, encourage the children to write down the prayer requests they heard in their group and/or spend time trying to hear God's voice.

God And Me

GOD MAKES YOU AND ME MIGHTY AT HOME!

LESSON SUMMARY: In this lesson we looked at ways God renews our strength when we get tired. We learned that praying and spending time being still and hearing His voice is one of the best ways He is able to give us the strength we need.

MEMORY VERSE: Philippians 4:13 - For I can do everything through Christ, who gives me strength.

IN THE CAR
- Talk with your family about eagles and what you learned about them in class. Pay attention to how other birds fly as you drive around town. What do you notice that's different?
- Talk with your family about things that are really easy for each of you to do and things that are difficult. What would it take for those difficult things to become easy?
- Talk about the different ways you can lose energy. In your body, and in your mind.

AT MEALTIMES
- Practice the memory verse for this unit with your family.
- Before you sit down to a meal, get your parents' permission to get online and search Bible verses about God's character. You can also use a concordance if your family has one. During meal times, talk about God's character.
- Talk about the role of a sidekick. What are ways we can be God's sidekick?

AT BEDTIME
- God wants to help us with everything we do. Pray with your family and ask God to show you how you can allow Him to help you with everyday tasks. Remind each other to let God help your family.
- Spend a few minutes each evening talking about things you appreciate or are grateful for from the day.
- Talk about the superhero that came to Sunday school this week. Why was he out of strength? How had he decided he was going to regain his strength at the end of class?

PRAYER REQUESTS:

© 2019 Angela E. Powell

Angela E. Powell

GOD MAKES YOU AND ME MIGHTY!

SUPPLIES NEEDED
Copies of take home sheet on page 142   Superhero cape   Superhero mask
Prayer Notebooks

LESSON 4: GOD GIVES ME STRENGTH
WELCOME
As you welcome children to class, have this question written on a white board, piece of paper, or ask the question to each child as you welcome them. Have the children find someone they don't know very well and discuss it.

Ice Breaker Question: What's the best thing that happened to you last week?

GAME
DON'T WAKE THE DRAGON
SUPPLIES: None

- Have the kids stand on one side of the room.
- Explain that you are a dragon and have taken over the classroom, but you're feeling the need for a nap. If the kids want to rescue the classroom, they'll have to run across the room after meeting certain requirements.
- Because the dragon is sleeping, the kids will not be able to talk.
- You can choose the requirements the kids have to fulfill. It can be something like lining up from shortest to tallest and running across the room in order, smallest shoe size to biggest shoe size, or even youngest to oldest. Remind them that they have to figure out the correct order without talking to each other.
- Give the kids time to figure out how to arrange themselves. When they think they have it figured out, have them run across the room.
- As the dragon, you can decide if they got the order right. If they didn't, the dragon can wake up and chase them back to the side of the room they started on.

LESSON 4: GOD GIVES ME STRENGTH
NOTE: The lessons in this unit use a superhero as an object lesson/skit. It is best if you can have someone dress up as the superhero, however if you don't have someone who can play the superhero, there are notes at the end on how you can modify this lesson.

NOTE: This lesson will work with the same superhero as last week, or a different one.

GOD MAKES YOU AND ME MIGHTY!

TEACHER: Good morning! We have [NAME] with us again today. Let's give him/her a warm welcome!

TEACHER: What's wrong [NAME]? You look a little grumpy today.

SH: Dark Thunder found my hide out yesterday and destroyed all my cars and weapons. I don't know how I'm going to save the city from him now.

TEACHER: But you're a superhero, you don't need cool cars and weapons to beat Dark Thunder.

SH: Maybe not, but having those things sure made it easier.

TEACHER: You know, there was a man in the Bible who had to learn how to be content with having very little at times. His name was Paul. I think you should hear what he had to say. Maybe it will help you.

SH: I don't know, I have a lot of work to do if I'm going to save the city.

TEACHER: What do you think kids? Should [NAME] stay for our lesson?

SH: All right, all right, I'll stay.

TEACHER: Great! I want to tell you a little bit about who Paul was. He was a missionary. Does anyone know what a missionary does?

SH: Is it someone who goes on secret missions like a superhero or spy?

TEACHER: Not exactly. A missionary is someone who travels to different places to tell people about God. A lot of missionaries don't make very much money and rely on gifts from people and churches to keep them going. The verses we're going to look at today are from a book called Philippians. This book is actually a letter to the Philippians that Paul wrote after the Philippians sent him a gift. Let's see what he had to say.

READ THE WORD
Have the kids follow along as the teacher or older kids read the following verses. **Philippians 4:10-13**

TEACHER: Paul tells the Philippians he has learned the secret of living in every situation. What is that secret?

Angela E. Powell

GOD MAKES YOU AND ME MIGHTY!

SH: *Shrugs and asks child next to him* Do you know?

TEACHER: The secret is our memory verse for this unit. "I can do all things through Christ who gives me strength".

SH: That can't be true.

TEACHER: Why not?

SH: Well, I can't make it rain. I can't turn into a rock, so I can't do everything.

TEACHER: I don't think that's what Paul meant. What do you guys think Paul meant when he said he could do everything through Christ?

TEACHER: Those are great answers! When we read a verse in the Bible we have to look at the other verses around it in order to understand what we're reading. Let's look at what Paul said in verses 10-12 again.

READ VERSES 10-12 again.

TEACHER: Paul is thanking the Philippians for the gift they sent him. Paul thanks them, but explains they don't need to worry about him because he has learned to be content with what he has. If he has plenty of food to eat, he's happy. If he doesn't have enough food to eat, he's happy. If he has lots of money he's happy, and if he only has a little money, he's happy.

TEACHER: Then Paul says the reason he can be happy no matter how little he has is because God gives him strength. So whatever Paul needs to do, God is going to give him the strength to get it done!

SH: So, if I trust God to give me strength to beat Dark Thunder, He'll give me the strength even though I don't have a cool car or any weapons to fight him with?

TEACHER: That's right! God makes you and me mighty, but sometimes the strength God gives us doesn't come from our muscles.

SH: What other kind of strength is there?

GOD MAKES YOU AND ME MIGHTY!

TEACHER: Let's say you have to give a speech at school, or be in a play, or get up in front of a crowd and sing a song. Some people don't have a problem with that, but others get stage fright. If you have a hard time performing on stage, you can trust God to give you the strength to get up there. That kind of strength could be called courage. Another type of strength could be energy. If you have a big project to do, God can give you enough rest at night so you have the energy to get through your day.

SH: So God's strength doesn't have anything to do with how much money we have, how many toys we have, or even how many friends we have?

TEACHER: That's right. God makes you and me mighty with what we have right here, right now.

SH: Instead of being grumpy about all my stuff being destroyed, I should be thankful because I always have God's strength with me. I just have to trust Him.

TEACHER: Exactly! We're memorizing Philippians 4:13 so we can be reminded that it's only trusting in God's strength, and not in our own that lets us be content no matter what our situation is. Our strength fails, but God's never does.

SH: I'm so glad I stayed today. It really does help to know God can give me the strength I need to save the city from Dark Thunder. I'm going to go pray and ask God for His strength right now! Bye kids!

ADAPTING THE LESSON FOR A ONE TEACHER CLASSROOM
If you only have one teacher available for this lesson, you can start the lesson by reminding the kids you've recently become a super hero. Or, if there is a different teacher for this lesson, explaining that you've just discovered you're a superhero. You can explain to the students you're a little grumpy because all your tools and gadgets were stolen and it's going to be harder to beat your enemies. Tell them you've been reading in the Bible about Paul and wanted to share with them what you've been learning and get their feedback. You would then proceed through the lesson and skip over the superhero comments.

MEMORY VERSE
SAY: Let's say our memory verse a few times.

Philippians 4:13 - For I can do everything through Christ, who gives me strength.

Angela E. Powell

GOD MAKES YOU AND ME MIGHTY!

PRAYER CIRCLES - "God With Me" Prayer

As the children learn to pray and hear God's voice, it can be helpful to give them each a notebook so they can keep track of what they hear and are praying for. Keep these notebooks in a safe place in class until you finish this curriculum. Encourage the kids to write down prayer requests they, or their peers have, on the take home sheet so they can be reminded to pray for those things during the week. For more information on this method of prayer, please look in the reference section on page 207.

- Hand each child a notebook they'll be able to use in class for the duration of this curriculum, and a pen or pencil. Tell the kids not to write in their notebooks until they are ready to write what they're hearing from the Lord.
- **Begin with Interactive Gratitude. Have the kids think of two or three things they're grateful for.** At first, they can start with things, but try to encourage them to list what they appreciate about their peers, teachers, parents, and other people they encounter every day.
- **Have the kids write down what they're thankful for in the form of a prayer.** ("God, today I'm thankful for...") Have them be as specific as possible. Instead of just saying they're thankful for their parents, have them come up with a specific reason they're thankful. The more specific they can get, the better.
- **Next, have them write down what they think God would say in response to the things they're grateful for.** This might be difficult at first if the kids don't know God's character very well. You may need to explain that God will always respond to us in love, and any judgmental, hurtful, or negative thoughts that come to their minds is not from God.
- **After the Interactive Gratitude is complete, have the kids take several deep breaths.** This will help calm their minds and bodies so they can better participate in the next portion.
- **Once everyone appears calm and relaxed, have them write down some things they want to pray about.** Have them write these things down as though God were sitting next to them having a conversation with Him. ("God, the bully at school is really bothering me.") To begin, it might be best to keep things simple. Have them pray for things on their radar: bullies at school, a subject in school they're struggling with, their parent's jobs, their siblings. At this point, we don't want them to go too deep until they really start understanding how to hear God's voice.
- If they have trouble coming up with subjects, give them some ideas such as praying they sleep well at night, or get up on time, or if they're willing they can pray for God to give them a desire to get to know Him. As long as the prayer is true for them they can pray about it. We don't want them to pray just to go through the motions.
- **Once they have one or two items, have them write as though God were responding to them. Begin with how God sees them.** For example, "I see you sitting in your classroom wondering what to pray about. I see how concerned you are about this issue. I see how worried you are about this."

GOD MAKES YOU AND ME MIGHTY!

- **Once they've written a sentence or two on that, move to "I hear you".** For example, "I hear you crying at night about this issue. I hear you telling me you want me to fix this. I hear you telling your parents how worried you are about the bully at school."
- **Next, have them write a couple sentences that start with "I understand how hard this is for you."** For example, "I understand how hard it is for you to go to school every day knowing there is a bully there, waiting." There may be some things the kids pray about that this wouldn't apply to. If that is the case, they can skip this step.
- **Next, have them write a couple of sentences that start with "I'm glad to be with you."** For example, "I'm glad to be with you right now as you tell me about this issue. I'm glad to be with you when you're crying in your bed at night. I'm glad to be with you even when you're struggling with negative emotions."
- **The last writing prompt to give them is, "I can do something about what you're going through."** This one might be harder if the kids don't understand God's character. In this case, God might respond by giving us a Bible verse reminding us of His goodness, His love, His faithfulness, etc. or He might remind us of a time in our past when we got through another difficult situation. Here is an example of what He might say, "I will help you continue to see more clearly who I am and what I've been doing in your life. I am protecting you. When you're feeling scared, remember I'm with you." Remind the kids that God will only say things that are loving, kind, and compassionate.
- **Finally, if anyone wants to share what God said to them, allow them some time for this.** This is an important step, and if you are able to spend time during the week before class practicing this method, it will help the kids be more comfortable with sharing if you are able to share from your own notebook.

Angela E. Powell

GOD MAKES YOU AND ME MIGHTY AT HOME!

LESSON SUMMARY: In this lesson we looked at Paul, who learned to trust God so well, he was never worried when money and food were tight, or when he had plenty because he knew God would take care of him no matter what. We looked at how we can learn to trust God in the same way.

MEMORY VERSE: Philippians 4:13 - For I can do everything through Christ, who gives me strength.

IN THE CAR
- Think about what you have that makes people like you. Talk it over with your family. Do you think people only like you because of the cool stuff you have, or is it because you are an awesome person?
- Talk about missionary work with your family. What kind of places do missionaries go? Are there places in the world where a missionary might be more comfortable than other places?
- Talk about how God's kind of strength is different from a superhero's.

AT MEALTIMES
- Practice the memory verse with your family.
- Discuss what it means to have character. What would tell you a person has good character? What about bad character? How can a person's character change over time?
- Read Acts 9 with your family. Discuss what Paul's character was like when he was Saul.

AT BEDTIME
- God wants to help us with everything we do. Pray with your family and ask God to show you how you can allow Him to help you with everyday tasks. Remind each other to let God help your family.
- Spend a few minutes each evening talking about things you appreciate or are grateful for from the day.
- Talk about things you've been wanting recently. Paul said he learned to be content with little and with much. Do you think you could be content not getting the things you've been wanting? Why or why not?

PRAYER REQUESTS:

God And Me

GOD MAKES YOU AND ME MIGHTY!

SUPPLIES NEEDED

Copies of take home sheet on page 149
Cardboard or Dollar store breast plates
Prayer Notebooks
Superhero cape
Hats
Superhero mask
Oversized shoes

LESSON 5: THE ARMOR OF GOD

WELCOME

As you welcome children to class, have this question written on a white board, piece of paper, or ask the question to each child as you welcome them. Have the children find someone they don't know very well and discuss it.

Ice Breaker Question: What is something that a ton of people are obsessed with, but you don't understand why?

GAME

ARMOR TAG

SUPPLIES: Cardboard or dollar store breast plates, Hats, Oversized shoes.

- Depending on how many kids you have, you may need to limit how many pieces of armor you use, or you may need to have multiple sets.
- For every 5-7 kids you have, pick 1 person to be a "Tagger".
- For every 5-7 kids you have, pick 1 person to be an "Armor Bearer". Have the armor bearers wear their piece of armor.
- Armor Bearers cannot be tagged.
- When a Tagger tags a child, that child must freeze.
- Armor Bearers will run up to any children who have been tagged and ask them if they want to be free. The child can answer yes or no. If they answer no, the Armor Bearer will move on and the child will have to remain frozen until another Armor Bearer asks them the question. If they say yes, the Armor bearer will remove their piece of armor and hand it to the frozen child.
- The frozen child becomes the new Armor Bearer and cannot be tagged, and the old Armor Bearer no longer has protection and can be tagged.
- Play until allotted time runs out.

Angela E. Powell

GOD MAKES YOU AND ME MIGHTY!

LESSON 5: THE ARMOR OF GOD

NOTE: The lessons in this unit use a superhero as an object lesson/skit. It is best if you can have someone dress up as the superhero, however if you don't have someone who can play the superhero, there are notes at the end on how you can modify this lesson.

NOTE: This lesson will work with the same superhero as last week, or a different one.

SUPERHERO: I have some exciting news to share! I got a brand new superhero cape!

TEACHER: That's great! Where is it?

SH: I'm wearing it.

TEACHER: Oh, it looks just like the old one.

SH: Yeah, well, this is my favorite color, but this is an armored cape. It can protect me from fire, and it doesn't rip or stain!

TEACHER: Sounds like a great piece of armor you have there.

SH: Oh, and there's a really cool thing about this cape. When I wrap it around myself, it makes me look like a big rock.

TEACHER: Really? Can we see?

SH: Of course! Here I go!

TEACHER: Um... superhero, I don't think your cape is working. You don't look like a big rock.

SH: What? I must have done it wrong. Let me try again.

TEACHER: Oh dear. It's still not working.

SH: *Takes cape off and stomps on it* I can't believe I spent $200 on that cape and it doesn't even work.

God And Me

GOD MAKES YOU AND ME MIGHTY!

TEACHER: Maybe you can return it and get your money back?

SH: OH, I will. I bet that sales guy was working for Scorpion.

TEACHER: Maybe you could try wearing God's armor instead of that cape?

SH: God has armor? How much does it cost?

TEACHER: It doesn't cost us any money, but it might cost us some time.

SH: What do you mean?

TEACHER: Let's read about God's armor in the Bible, then I'll explain.

READ THE WORD

Have the kids follow along as the teacher or older kids read the following verses. **Ephesians 6:10-18**

TEACHER: As a child of God our enemies aren't other people. God wants us to love and be kind to everyone, but the devil wants us to be mad at each other and argue. Most people don't realize it's the devil who's encouraging us to be mad and stay mad at people. So God gave us some armor to help.

ASK: The first piece of armor is the belt of truth. What do you think that means?

SH: It's a belt that's also a lie detector so you can tell when the enemy is lying to you!

TEACHER: No! The belt of truth reminds us to always tell the truth. Lies are from the devil. He makes us think telling the truth will be scary, but God always wants us to be truthful.

ASK: The next piece of armor is the body armor of God's righteousness. Does anyone know what righteousness means?

TEACHER: It means acting in a way that's right. So God's righteousness is when we act the way God wants us to.

ASK: What are some ways God wants us to act?

SH: Love people. Obey our parents. Be kind to people. Tell the truth.

Angela E. Powell

GOD MAKES YOU AND ME MIGHTY!

TEACHER: Right, so when we do those things, we're putting on God's body armor. Next we have the shoes of peace. The Bible says this peace comes from the good news.

SH: What is the good news?

TEACHER: The good news is that Jesus came to save us from sin by dying on the cross and coming back to life three days later.

SH: Wait a minute. Are we supposed to wear Bible's on our feet? Because I don't think that would make very good armor.

TEACHER: No. We're supposed to remember what Jesus did for us, because that will bring us peace. Next we have the shield of faith.

SH: Oh, like Captain America's shield?

TEACHER: Not quite. This is a shield of faith. Faith is trusting in God completely. Even when it looks like things aren't going to work out like you thought they would.

SH: Do any of you kids think this sounds like really weird armor?

TEACHER: Stay with me. We have two pieces left. The next is the helmet of salvation.

SH: Finally, something that makes sense! The helmet of salvation saves your head from getting injured!

TEACHER: Kind of. It's supposed to protect your thoughts.

SH: ...from what?

TEACHER: It helps you know when a thought is yours, God's voice, or the enemy's voice. We practice wearing the helmet of salvation when we pray, read our Bibles, and practice hearing and knowing God's voice.

SH: That's cool.

TEACHER: The last piece of armor is the sword of the spirit.

GOD MAKES YOU AND ME MIGHTY!

SH: A ghost hunting sword!

TEACHER: No, no, no. The sword of the spirit is our Bible.

SH: What? The Bible isn't a sword. It's a book!

TEACHER: Yes, that's true, but the words inside are just as powerful as a sword.

SH: Wait. I think I'm starting to understand now. God's armor isn't really something we put on, it's things we do. Like telling the truth, doing things that are right, trusting in God, and reading our Bibles.

TEACHER: That's exactly right! Now do you see why God's armor costs us time, but not money?

SH: No, do you kids understand what that means?

TEACHER: Those are great answers. It takes time to do the right things. It takes time to read our Bibles. It takes time to learn how to trust God. We can't put on God's armor if we aren't willing to take the time.

SH: I get it now. If I take the time to put on God's armor, then God will help me be mighty!

TEACHER: That's right! Not only will God help you be mighty, but you'll get better and better at hearing His voice. Your relationship with Him will grow too!

ADAPTING THE LESSON FOR A ONE TEACHER CLASSROOM

If you only have one teacher available for this lesson, you can start the lesson by reminding the kids you've recently become a super hero. Or, if there is a different teacher for this lesson, explaining that you've just discovered you're a superhero. Explain that you just got a new cape and show them how it can turn into a rock. Ask them what they think of the capes new trick. If they don't tell you it doesn't work, you can say a superhero friend said it wasn't working but you didn't believe them, then ask the kids if it worked. Share how you've been reading about God's armor in the Bible and are thinking of trading your cape in for God's armor. You would then proceed through the lesson and skip over the superhero comments.

GOD MAKES YOU AND ME MIGHTY!

MEMORY VERSE

SAY: Let's say our memory verse a few times.

Philippians 4:13 - For I can do everything through Christ, who gives me strength.

PRAYER CIRCLES - Groups

As the children are learning to pray and hear God's voice, it can be helpful to give them each a notebook where they can write down what they're hearing and keep track of what they've been praying for. Keep these notebooks in class until you finish this curriculum. Encourage the kids to write down prayer requests they, or their peers have on the take home sheet so they can be reminded to pray for those things during the week.

- Have kids get into groups of three or four with at least one older child or leader in each group.
- Have the kids share their prayer requests with the others in their group.
- Encourage each child to pray for one of the prayer requests presented.
- If no one has prayer requests or there aren't enough for everyone to pray about, give them suggestions such as, praying for a good, safe week for everyone or God would bring in more kids.
- If some groups finish before others, encourage the children to write down the prayer requests they heard in their group and/or spend time trying to hear God's voice.

God And Me

GOD MAKES YOU AND ME MIGHTY AT HOME!

LESSON SUMMARY: Today we learned about God's armor. We discovered why God gives us armor and what its purpose is. We learned that God's armor isn't physical, but tools He's given us to help us as we walk through life.

MEMORY VERSE: Philippians 4:13 - For I can do everything through Christ, who gives me strength.

IN THE CAR
- Talk about the armor of God. Can you remember all the pieces of the armor and what they're for?
- Talk about how God's armor is different than the armor someone in the military, or a police officer would wear.
- Sometimes we create our own armor to protect ourselves. We might wear certain clothes because they give us confidence, or wear makeup, or we might keep to ourselves and ignore people. Discuss how these types of armor can hurt us instead of protect us.

AT MEALTIMES
- Practice the memory verse with your family.
- Talk about the belt of truth. How can you remind yourself to tell the truth no matter what?
- Talk about the shoes of peace. If the Bible can remind us what Jesus did for us, and if that knowledge gives us peace, then what do we need to do in order to put on the shoes of peace?

AT BEDTIME
- Talk about how God's armor costs us time and not money. Why would the sword of the spirit, the Bible, cost us time?
- Discuss why it's important to put on the armor of God every day. How do we accomplish this?
- Talk about the superhero that came to class during Sunday school. Why was he so confused about the armor of God?

PRAYER REQUESTS:

Angela E. Powell

UNIT 5

UNIT THEME: GOD CAN TALK TO YOU AND ME

This unit focuses on prayer. We will learn that prayer is a two way street, not a one way street. The children will have opportunities to develop their praying and listening skills during the prayer circle time of each lesson. Because this is such an important skill to learn, the lessons are shorter on purpose in order to allow time for hands-on application.

Lesson 1: The Lord's Prayer
This first lesson will dig into the Lord's Prayer in order to understand how Jesus showed us to pray. The rest of the lessons will take one of the four points we find in the Lord's Prayer and expand on it.

Lesson 2: P.R.A.Y. PRAISE
In this lesson the kids will discover a part of prayer is praising God. This helps us get in the right frame of mind to hear the voice of the Lord, and helps calm our thoughts so we can focus on what He wants to say.

Lesson 3: P.R.A.Y. REVEAL
In this lesson the children will discover God reveals Himself to us through prayer, slowly, over time because He doesn't want to overwhelm us. They'll learn that just like their teachers in school teach them certain steps in math before others, God reveals certain things about Himself as we spend time with Him and learn about Him.

Lesson 4: P.R.A.Y. ASSIST
In this lesson the kids will learn that part of prayer is asking God for what we need, but it's only a small part and sometimes we need to keep praying and listening in order to hear God's answer.

Lesson 5: P.R.A.Y. YIELD
In this lesson we'll look at what it means to yield to the Lord. We'll explain what yield means and offer several examples of how yielding works and what its purpose is. We'll then learn why God asks us to yield to Him and how that works in prayer.

Optional Videos For This Unit: https://bit.ly/2E4aBEj

GOD CAN TALK TO YOU AND ME!

SUPPLIES NEEDED

- Copies of take home sheet on page 156
- Mod Podge waterproof sealer
- Lined paper, or small notebooks
- Instruction booklet from any product
- Song: "That's Why We Praise Him"
- River stones
- Paper plates
- Foam paint brushes
- Kid's being tempted video
- Prayer Notebooks
- Colored Sharpie markers
- Popcorn
- Pens or pencils

LESSON 1: THE LORD'S PRAYER

WELCOME

As you welcome children to class, have this question written on a white board, piece of paper, or ask the question to each child as you welcome them. Have the children find someone they don't know very well and discuss it.

Ice Breaker Question: What is one of your favorite smells?

GAME

POPCORN TOSS

SUPPLIES: Bag of popcorn

- Divide kids in two equal groups. Have them stand in two lines, facing each other ten feet apart.
- Each child will need to face another child as the children will be tossing popcorn to each other.
- Give all the kids in the first row one piece of popcorn. At your signal, have the kids toss the popcorn to the person across from them in the second row.
- Record how many successful catches there were on a board or piece of paper.
- Make sure each child in the second row has a piece of popcorn. Have them take one step forward. Make sure everyone stays in a line and there aren't some children closer to the other line than others.
- Have the kids toss the popcorn and again record the number of successful catches.
- Now make sure each child in the first line has a piece of popcorn and have them take a step forward. Repeat the process until the kids are able to drop the popcorn in each other's hands.
- Explain that a relationship with God is similar to the game. When we are not in frequent communication with God, it can be hard to know when we're hearing His voice, and what we should be doing, but when we talk to Him a lot, we learn to hear His voice and we know Him better.

Angela E. Powell

GOD CAN TALK TO YOU AND ME!

LESSON 1: THE LORD'S PRAYER
NOTE: This lesson uses the NLT version.
Hold up the instruction booklet.
ASK: Do you know what this is?

SAY: It's an instruction booklet for _____. It shows me how this product works, how to put it together, how to clean it and care for it, and some things I can do if it doesn't work the way it's supposed to. I think it would be nice if there were instructions on how to make friends or how to study the Bible.

ASK: What part of life do you wish had an instruction booklet? Did you know the Bible gives us instructions on all kinds of things?

SAY: Today we're going to look at God's instructions on how to pray.

READ THE WORD
Have the kids follow along as the teacher or older kids read the following verses. **Matthew 6:9-13**

SAY: Some of these verses use words that might be hard for us to understand. Let's look at some of them.

SAY: The first line says, "Our Father in heaven, may Your name be kept holy."

ASK: What do you think that means?

SAY: First of all, it starts by saying "Father" instead of "God" or "Lord". God wants us to talk to Him like we would with a relative we're comfortable talking to about anything.

SAY: The word "holy" means to keep pure or to set apart as important. So, the first thing God wants us to do is remember to put Him first. To remember all the things He's done for us and given us.

ASK: How do we do that?

SAY: We thank Him. We remember, then we thank Him. We call this praise. Songs can remind us of things we can thank God for. Let's listen to one right now.

God And Me

GOD CAN TALK TO YOU AND ME!

Watch a music video or listen to the song, "That's Why We Praise Him". There is a link on the overview page where you can find videos for this unit or you can use your own.

SAY: If we ever need help figuring out what to thank God for, we can always start by thanking Him for dying for our sins. The next line says, "May Your kingdom come soon. May Your will be done on earth, as it is in heaven."

ASK: What do you think it means when it says, "Your will be done"?

SAY: God has a plan for every person on earth, but He gave all of us something called "free will", which means we can choose how we'll live our lives. But God is asking us to pray that we will all choose to follow God's will for our lives. In other words, He wants us to want what He wants. The more we choose to live God's plan for our lives, the more we'll get to know who God is. He'll reveal, or show, more of Himself to us.

SAY: The next line is, "Give us today, the food we need."

ASK: Do we need a bag of chips every day?

SAY: No! We need food that will keep us healthy. We may *want* a bag of chips every day, but God only promises to give us what we need. This isn't only talking about food either. This could mean a place to live, clothes to wear, or even a job when you're old enough to get one. So God wants us to ask Him for things we need.

SAY: The next part says, "Forgive us our sins as we have forgiven those who have sinned against us."

ASK: What does it mean to forgive? Have you ever said, or heard someone say, "I'll never forgive them."?

SAY: What they're really saying is they choose to hold onto the anger and hurt they feel. Every time that person is thought about or seen, we choose to remember how angry or hurt they made us feel. When we forgive someone we choose not to be angry or hurt anymore. Instead, when we see them, we can be kind to them because we choose to let go of the anger and pain.

SAY: God wants us to come to Him anytime we do something that causes Him pain so He can forgive us. He also wants us to remember that since He is willing to forgive all of our sins, we should be willing to forgive anyone who hurts us.

Angela E. Powell

GOD CAN TALK TO YOU AND ME!

SAY: The last part of the Lord's Prayer says, "Don't let us yield to temptation, but rescue us from the evil one."

ASK: What does it mean to yield?

SAY: It means "to give into". So God is telling us to pray that we won't give into temptation.

ASK: What does it mean to be tempted?

Show a video of kids being tempted, and/or explain. There is a link on the overview page where you can find videos for this unit or you can use your own.

SAY: Temptation is a desire to do something wrong. For example, if you get home from school before your mom and dad and the rule is you have to do your homework and chores before watching T.V., you might be tempted to watch T.V. because how would they ever find out?

SAY: God wants us to pray and ask for His help in resisting, or saying no to things that tempt us.

SAY: Let's review. God wants us to PRAISE Him when we pray. He wants to REVEAL more of Himself to us through prayer. He wants us to ask Him for things we need and for help or ASSISTANCE. And finally, He wants us to pray that we will choose His way over our own. In other words, He wants us to YIELD to Him.

SAY: We're going to look at those four things in the next four lessons. To help you remember, think: PRAY. Praise, Reveal, Assist, and Yield.

HANDS-ON ACTIVITY

SUPPLIES: River stones, Colored Sharpies, Mod Podge waterproof sealer, Foam paint brushes, Paper plates

- The stones should be rinsed and dried before class.
- Let each child choose a stone.
- Have them write "PRAY" on the stone with the markers and let them decorate the stone.
- When they are done, let the kids paint a thin layer of mod podge over their stones to seal in the marker.
- Let the stones dry on a paper plate with the child's name on it.
- Leave the stone in the classroom, the kids will take 5 stones home at the end of the unit.

God And Me

GOD CAN TALK TO YOU AND ME!

MEMORY VERSE

SAY: Let's say our memory verse a few times.

Matthew 6:9-13 – Our Father in heaven, may Your name be kept holy. May Your kingdom come soon. May Your will be done on earth, as it is in heaven. Give us today the food we need, and forgive us our sins as we have forgiven those who sin against us. And don't let us yield to temptation, but rescue us from the evil one.

PRAYER CIRCLES - Modified Sozo

As the children are learning to pray and hear God's voice, it can be helpful to give them each a notebook where they can write down what they're hearing and keep track of what they've been praying for. Keep these notebooks in class until you finish this curriculum. Encourage the kids to write down prayer requests they, or their peers have on the take home sheet so they can be reminded to pray for those things during the week.

SAY: We're going to do something a little different for our prayer time for the next several weeks. Instead of getting into groups to pray, we're going to pray on our own and practice listening for God's voice.

SAY: I want you to start by thinking of one thing you can thank God for, and I want you to write it down or draw a picture of it.

Give them about 2 minutes to do this.

SAY: Now, I want you to close your eyes and in your mind, ask God what He likes about you. Write down, or draw a picture of the first thing that comes to your mind. When you're done writing down or drawing that answer, ask God to give you an image of what He's like. Then ask God how He feels about your right now. Write down, or draw pictures of all your answers.

Give the kids 5 minutes unless they get restless and distracting. Don't have the kid's share this week unless they want to tell you personally.

GOD CAN TALK TO YOU AND ME AT HOME!

LESSON SUMMARY: Today we read the Lord's Prayer from Matthew 6:9-13. This is also our memory verse for this unit. We broke the prayer into four parts. For the next four weeks, we will talk about each of these in detail. We discussed what words like "forgiven", "tempted", and "yield" mean and came up with the acronym P.R.A.Y. to help us remember God's instructions on how to pray. Praise, Reveal, Assist, and Yield. We also talked about how God gives us free will, but He wants us to choose His will for our lives. We will talk about this more when we discuss the "Y" in our acronym.

MEMORY VERSE: Matthew 6:9-13 – Our Father in heaven, may Your name be kept holy. May Your kingdom come soon. May Your will be done on earth, as it is in heaven. Give us today the food we need, and forgive us our sins as we have forgiven those who sin against us. And don't let us yield to temptation, but rescue us from the evil one.

IN THE CAR
Discuss the lesson with your kids. Some questions you might ask them are:
- How did the lesson make you feel?
- What instructions did God give us about prayer?
- What is free will?

AT MEALTIMES
- Read Psalm 95 and Psalm 100 together. Discuss the reasons for "giving thanks".
- Read Psalm 3 together. Discuss what David asks God to do for him, and what he gives thanks for.
- Read Psalm 84 together. After reading, discuss why this Psalm suggests that yielding to God's will might be better than any plans we might make on our own.

AT BEDTIME
Use the example of the Lord's Prayer and pray with your kids before they go to bed.
- Begin with Praise, or thanking the Lord.
- Ask Him to Reveal something to you about your day. This could be as simple as asking, "How were You with us today, Lord?" or "What do you want me to know about today?"
- Next, ask Him to Assist you and/or your children with something that's a struggle. This could be anything from helping a child to get up on time in the morning, to dealing with the loss of a family member.
- Finally, ask God to bring you all to a place where you want to yield to His will for your lives.

PRAYER REQUESTS:

God And Me

GOD CAN TALK TO YOU AND ME!

SUPPLIES NEEDED

Copies of take home sheet on page 161	River stones	Colored Sharpie markers
Mod Podge waterproof sealer	Foam paint brushes	Paper
Pens or pencils	Paper plates	Prayer notebooks

LESSON 2: P.R.A.Y. PRAISE

WELCOME

As you welcome children to class, have this question written on a white board, piece of paper, or ask the question to each child as you welcome them. Have the children find someone they don't know very well and discuss it.

Ice Breaker Question: If you had to change your name, what would you change it to?

GAME

PAPER PRAYER TELEPHONE

SUPPLIES: Paper, Pens or pencils

- Before class, fold several pieces of paper into fans, so each section of fan is about one inch.
- Hand out the fans and pens or pencils to each child.
- Have each child write a short prayer on the first fan section. Allow about a minute for this.
- Have the kids pass their paper to the right. The kids will read the prayer written on the first section, then draw a picture of that prayer on the second section. When they're done, they'll fold the paper so only their picture can be seen. Allow 2 minutes for this.
- Have the kids pass the paper to the right again. The kids will only look at the picture the last person drew. They'll write down a prayer that goes along with the drawing. Allow 1 minute.
- Again, have the kids fold the paper, so only the written part can be seen and the first two sections are hidden. Have them pass the paper to the right.
- Continue the pattern until the last section is filled. Then have the kids open the papers and see if anyone had the same prayer at the bottom and the top.

LESSON 2: P.R.A.Y. PRAISE

SAY: Imagine this: Tomorrow when you wake up, you only have the things you thanked God for today.

ASK: What you would thank Him for? What if half the things you thanked Him for, disappeared tomorrow? Would you still be thankful for them? Why or why not?

Angela E. Powell

GOD CAN TALK TO YOU AND ME!

SAY: Today I want to look at three places in the Bible where people praised God, and another place that gives us more instructions about how to pray.

SAY: First, let's look at a Psalm of David.

ASK: Does anyone know who David was?

SAY: David killed Goliath when he was a boy and grew up to become king of Israel. He is called a man after God's own heart because he spent a lot of time praying to God and knew God really well. Many of the 150 Psalms were written by David. Let's look at one of them.

READ THE WORD
Have the kids follow along as the teacher or older kids read the following verses. **Psalm 63**

ASK: Did David ask for anything in this prayer?

SAY: No. David says at the end, "Those who want to kill me will be destroyed…" He didn't ask God to destroy them, but David knew God would protect him and he was thanking God for that. David is a good example of what a close relationship with Jesus is like because David made God more important than anything else for most of his life.

SAY: Now, let's look at a prayer Jesus prayed.

READ THE WORD
Have the kids follow along as the teacher or older kids read the following verses. **Matthew 15:32-38**

SAY: Jesus saw these people needed to eat, but there was not enough food to go around and no store close by. Last week we talked about how God will give us what we need, but He may not give us what we want. These people needed food, so Jesus knew His Father would provide.

SAY: It doesn't tell us what Jesus prayed, it just says He gave thanks, then started passing out the food, which multiplied miraculously.

ASK: What do you think Jesus gave thanks for?

GOD CAN TALK TO YOU AND ME!

SAY: Probably for the bread and fish the boy brought, maybe thanking God for providing what the people needed. This was a pretty simple prayer. Just like when we pray at meal times. Jesus didn't have to ask for a miracle because He knew God would provide what the people needed.

SAY: Next we're going to look at a book called Habakkuk. Habakkuk was a prophet. This book of the Bible only has three chapters and the whole book is a conversation Habakkuk has with God about the people of Israel, who were about to be punished for disobeying the Lord. At the very end of the book, Habakkuk praises God. Let's take a look.

READ THE WORD
Have the kids follow along as the teacher or older kids read the following verses. **Habakkuk 3:17-19**

SAY: Here, Habakkuk is telling God that if God were to take everything away from the Israelites, Habakkuk would still praise God and thank him. Habakkuk knew if God was punishing Israel it was because the people were doing bad things and needed to be corrected. But he also knew that once God had given them their consequence, He would still love them, still give them what they needed, and would still send Jesus to save us from our sins.

SAY: So even when life doesn't look very good, we can still find things to thank Jesus for. Before we make our prayer stone for today, I want to look at some more instructions the Bible gives us about prayer.

READ THE WORD
Have the kids follow along as the teacher or older kids read the following verses. **1 Thessalonians 5:16-18**

SAY: God wants us to always be looking for things to be thankful for. He also wants us to live a life of prayer.

ASK: What do you think that means?

SAY: Prayer is a fancy name for talking. God wants us to live our lives constantly talking to Him. Anytime you take a walk down the street, look around and find things you can thank Him for. See a pretty flower? Thank God for it. Enjoying a warm day? Thank God for it. Make talking to God an important part of your day.

Angela E. Powell

GOD CAN TALK TO YOU AND ME!

HANDS-ON ACTIVITY

SUPPLIES: River stones, Colored Sharpies, Mod Podge waterproof sealer, Foam paint brushes, Paper plates

- The stones should be rinsed and dried before class. Let each child choose a stone.
- Have them write "PRAISE" on the stone with the markers and let them decorate the stone.
- When they're done, let the kids paint a thin layer of mod podge over their stones.
- Let the stones dry on a paper plate with the child's name on it.
- Leave the stone in the classroom, the kids will take all 5 stones home at the end of the unit.

MEMORY VERSE

SAY: Let's say our memory verse a few times.

Matthew 6:9-13 – Our Father in heaven, may Your name be kept holy. May Your kingdom come soon. May Your will be done on earth, as it is in heaven. Give us today the food we need, and forgive us our sins as we have forgiven those who sin against us. And don't let us yield to temptation, but rescue us from the evil one.

PRAYER CIRCLES - Modified Sozo

As the children are learning to pray and hear God's voice, it can be helpful to give them each a notebook where they can write down what they're hearing and keep track of what they've been praying for. Keep these notebooks in class until you finish this curriculum. Encourage the kids to write down prayer requests they, or their peers have on the take home sheet so they can be reminded to pray for those things during the week.

SAY: We're going to do something a little different for our prayer time. Instead of getting into groups to pray, we're going to pray on our own and practice listening for God's voice.

SAY: I want you to start by thinking of two things you can thank God for, and I want you to write them down or draw a picture of them. **Give them about 2 minutes to do this.**

SAY: Now, I want you to close your eyes and in your mind, ask God what He wants you to know about prayer. Ask Jesus how He feels about your right now, and ask Jesus to show you and image of what He's like. Write down or draw a picture of the first thing that comes to your mind for each question.

Give the kids 5 minutes unless they get restless and distracting. Don't have the kid's share this week unless they want to tell you personally.

God And Me

GOD CAN TALK TO YOU AND ME AT HOME!

LESSON SUMMARY: Today we looked at three places in the Bible, **(Psalm 63, Matthew 15:36, and Habakkuk 3:17-19)** where someone prayed a prayer of thanksgiving. We looked at what those people were going through at the time and learned it doesn't matter if life is good and easy, or hard and a struggle, we can always find something to thank God for.

MEMORY VERSE: Matthew 6:9-13 – Our Father in heaven, may Your name be kept holy. May Your kingdom come soon. May Your will be done on earth, as it is in heaven. Give us today the food we need, and forgive us our sins as we have forgiven those who sin against us. And don't let us yield to temptation, but rescue us from the evil one.

IN THE CAR
Discuss the lesson with your kids. Some questions you might ask them are:
- How did the lesson make you feel?
- What did you learn about praising, or thanking God?
- When should we praise God?
- What should we praise God for?

AT MEALTIMES
- Read 1 Thessalonians 5:16-18 together. Discuss ways we can "rejoice always" even when we're sad, upset, or discouraged.
- This passage also mentions it's God's will for us to rejoice always, pray continually, and give thanks in all circumstances. This is one way we can yield to God's will for our lives. Discuss situations where this could be easy and situations where it could be difficult.

AT BEDTIME
Help your children learn to hear God's voice. Take five minutes and ask God something simple, then wait for His reply. It's good practice to write down what you hear so you can refer back to it. Some questions you could ask God are:
- What was your favorite part about today?
- Where were you when I was doing _____?
- How do you feel about me right now?
- What do you want me to know about _____?

PRAYER REQUESTS:

© 2019 Angela E. Powell

Angela E. Powell

GOD CAN TALK TO YOU AND ME!

SUPPLIES NEEDED

Copies of take home sheet on page 167	Butcher paper	Strong tape
Colored pencils or crayons	River stones	Colored Sharpie markers
Mod Podge waterproof sealer	Foam paint brushes	Paper plates
Prayer notebooks	Pens or pencils	

LESSON 3: P.R.A.Y. REVEAL

WELCOME

As you welcome children to class, have this question written on a white board, piece of paper, or ask the question to each child as you welcome them. Have the children find someone they don't know very well and discuss it.

Ice Breaker Question: What do you wish your brain was better at doing?

GAME

GRAFFITI PRAYER WALL

SUPPLIES: Butcher paper, Strong tape, Colored pencils or crayons

- Before class, hang a long strip of butcher paper on the wall.
- Have the kids write prayer requests, and things they can thank God for on the butcher paper. They can also draw pictures of these things.
- Give them 10-15 minutes to decorate as much of the paper as they can.

LESSON 3: P.R.A.Y. REVEAL

Write the following math problem on the board, or a piece of paper that can be passed around:
$3 + 10x - 5 = (a + 1) * x - 2$

ASK: How many of you could solve this problem? How many of you think this doesn't even look like real math?

SAY: When you were in kindergarten, or first grade, you started learning how to add two numbers together. Then you learned how to subtract two numbers. Once you learned that, you were taught how to add and subtract more than two numbers and then two and three digit numbers.

SAY: The older you get, the more math you'll learn, but you can't learn the harder stuff if you don't learn the basics first. You could say more math is revealed to you the more you understand what you've already learned.

God And Me

GOD CAN TALK TO YOU AND ME!

SAY: God is the same way. The more time we spend with God, the more He'll reveal Himself to us. In other words, the more time we spend with Him the better we'll know Him. But we won't just learn who God is, we'll also learn what His plan for us is, and what He wants to do in our lives. He wants to reveal all kinds of things to us, but we have to spend time getting to know Him first. The best way to do that is through prayer.

SAY: Today we're going to look at three Bible stories. In one, God reveals himself, in another, God reveals some information that saves His people, and finally, God reveals His plan to help a servant stop being afraid.

ASK: Who knows who Moses is?

SAY: Moses was born in Egypt at a time when the Hebrew people were slaves. He is also the man God used to bring the ten plagues on Egypt so the Hebrews could escape slavery. Moses led the Hebrew people until they reached the land God promised them. While they were wandering in the desert, God met with Moses a lot. He gave Moses the Ten Commandments. You would think Moses knew God pretty well since they spent so much time talking, and you'd be right, but Moses knew there was even more to know about God. Let's read what Moses asked God.

READ THE WORD

Have the kids follow along as the teacher or older kids read the following verses. **Exodus 33:12-14, 17-18, 34:5-8**

SAY: Moses wanted to know God better and asked God to reveal more of Himself to Moses. And the Lord did exactly what Moses asked. He told Moses some information about who He is. He's the God of compassion and mercy, He's slow to anger, filled with unfailing love and faithfulness, He forgives, and then He tells Moses how He deals with sin.

ASK: I think Moses was impressed don't you?

SAY: If any of us ask God to show us more of who He is, God will do it, you just have to be willing to listen for His voice. Let's look at another time the Israelites were forced to leave their land and work for another country.

ASK: Who knows who Daniel is? Remember the story of Daniel in the Lion's Den?

Angela E. Powell

GOD CAN TALK TO YOU AND ME!

SAY: This is the same Daniel. The king, Nebuchadnezzar, had a dream one night and he was sure God was trying to give him a message, but he wasn't sure what the message was. So he asked the wise men in his kingdom to tell him the meaning of the dream, but when the wise men asked the king what the dream was, he refused to tell them. Let's read about it.

READ THE WORD
Have the kids follow along as the teacher or older kids read the following verses. **Daniel 2:5-7, 14-19**

SAY: The king was going to kill the wise men if they couldn't tell him what the dream was, and what it meant. Daniel was one of these wise men. He needed help! So he prayed and asked God to reveal the dream and it's meaning to him, and God did.

ASK: What did Moses and Daniel do after God revealed something to them?

SAY: They worshiped, or praised. They thanked God for the revelation.

SAY: If we're facing something hard or impossible, we can pray and ask God to show, or reveal, the way out of that situation and He will do it. But we have to be in relationship with Him and learn how to hear His voice first or we may not be certain we've really heard Him.

SAY: The last story we're going to look at is in the book of 2 Kings. The king of Syria started a war with Israel. God kept telling the prophet Elisha all of Syria's plans and Elisha would tell the king what God said, which meant God was helping Israel win the war.

SAY: This made the king of Syria very angry and eventually he found out what Elisha was doing, so he decided he was going to kill Elisha. Let's read what happened.

READ THE WORD
Have the kids follow along as the teacher or older kids read the following verses. **2 Kings 6:14-18**

SAY: The king of Syria sent his whole army to Elisha's house! When the servant went out he was really scared, but Elisha wasn't. God revealed something to Elisha, but the servant didn't know it. So Elisha prayed and asked God to show the servant what God had shown Elisha. God sent an army of angels to protect Elisha and there were more angels than there were men in the Syrian army!

GOD CAN TALK TO YOU AND ME!

SAY: When we're afraid, we can ask God to show us He is bigger than the thing we fear, and He will. God wants to show us who He is, but He's such a big God that if He showed us who He is all at once, we would be overwhelmed. Instead, He reveals Himself to us a little at a time as we choose to get to know Him and learn about Him.

HANDS-ON ACTIVITY

SUPPLIES: River stones, Colored Sharpies, Mod Podge waterproof sealer, Foam paint brushes, Paper plates

- The stones should be rinsed and dried before class.
- Let each child choose a stone.
- Have them write "REVEAL" on the stone with the markers and let them decorate the stone.
- When they are done, let the kids paint a thin layer of mod podge over their stones.
- Let the stones dry on a paper plate with the child's name on it.
- Leave the stone in the classroom, the kids will take all 5 stones home at the end of the unit.

MEMORY VERSE

SAY: Let's say our memory verse a few times.

Matthew 6:9-13 – Our Father in heaven, may Your name be kept holy. May Your kingdom come soon. May Your will be done on earth, as it is in heaven. Give us today the food we need, and forgive us our sins as we have forgiven those who sin against us. And don't let us yield to temptation, but rescue us from the evil one.

PRAYER CIRCLES - Modified Sozo

As the children are learning to pray and hear God's voice, it can be helpful to give them each a notebook where they can write down what they're hearing and keep track of what they've been praying for. Keep these notebooks in class until you finish this curriculum. Encourage the kids to write down prayer requests they, or their peers have on the take home sheet so they can be reminded to pray for those things during the week.

SAY: Find a spot to sit where you can pray on your own and practice listening for God's voice. I want you to start by thinking of two things you can thank God for, write them down or draw a picture of them.

Give them about 2 minutes to do this.

GOD CAN TALK TO YOU AND ME!

SAY: Now, I want you to close your eyes and in your mind, ask God what He wants to reveal to you today. Ask God what He likes about you, and ask God what He likes about your family. Write down, or draw a picture of the first thing that comes to your mind for each question.

Give the kids 5 minutes unless they get restless and distracting. Encourage the kids to share what they've heard from the past three weeks. When we share what God is telling us, it encourages and helps us determine if what we heard lines up with the Bible or not. It can be helpful if you are able to take time during the week to hear from the Lord yourself about these questions so you can share with the kids.

GOD CAN TALK TO YOU AND ME AT HOME!

LESSON SUMMARY: Today we talked about how God wants to reveal more of Himself to us and how He goes about doing that through conversation with Him. We looked at when Moses asked to see God's face as he led the people of Israel in the wilderness to show that God wants us to get to know Him personally. We also looked at when God revealed a king's dream and the meaning of it to Daniel to save his life and the lives of the other wise men living in Babylon at the time. Then we looked at the story of Elisha whose house was surrounded by an enemy army. His servant was scared, but God reveled to them God's army of angels, more numerous than the enemy's army.

MEMORY VERSE: Matthew 6:9-13 – Our Father in heaven, may Your name be kept holy. May Your kingdom come soon. May Your will be done on earth, as it is in heaven. Give us today the food we need, and forgive us our sins as we have forgiven those who sin against us. And don't let us yield to temptation, but rescue us from the evil one.

IN THE CAR
Discuss the lesson with your kids. Some questions you might ask them are:
- How did the lesson make you feel?
- What did you learn about God today?
- How does God reveal Himself to us?

AT MEALTIMES
- Read the story of Moses asking to see Gods face. Discuss why God reveals Himself to us a little at a time. **Exodus 22:12-14, 18-23**
- Read the story of Elisha. What did Elisha know that the servant didn't? **2 Kings 6:14-18**

AT BEDTIME
Use the example of the Lord's Prayer and pray with your kids before they go to bed.
- Begin with Praise, or thanking the Lord.
- Ask Him to Reveal something to you about your day. This could be as simple as asking, "How were you with us today, Lord?" or "What do you want me to know about today?"
- Next, ask Him to Assist you and/or your children with something that's a struggle. This could be anything from helping a child to get up on time in the morning, to dealing with the loss of a family member.
- Finally, ask God to bring you all to a place where you want to yield to His will for your lives.

PRAYER REQUESTS:

Angela E. Powell

GOD CAN TALK TO YOU AND ME!

SUPPLIES NEEDED
- Copies of take home sheet on page 173
- Mod Podge waterproof sealer
- Prayer notebooks
- Colored pencils, markers, or crayons
- River stones
- Foam paint brushes
- Pens or pencils
- Colored Sharpie markers
- Paper plates
- Paper

LESSON 4: P.R.A.Y. ASSIST
WELCOME
As you welcome children to class, have this question written on a white board, piece of paper, or ask the question to each child as you welcome them. Have the children find someone they don't know very well and discuss it.

Ice Breaker Question: What is something you are certain you'll never experience?

GAME
PRAYER DOODLES
SUPPLIES: Paper, Colored pencils, markers, or crayons
- Give each person a piece of paper.
- Let them write down a prayer request or praise.
- Have them decorate the letters, and the space around their prayer, but have them pray about that thing as they doodle.

LESSON 4: P.R.A.Y. ASSIST
ASK: How many of you have ever pressed one of those buttons that makes doors open for people? They're fun to use right? Are they meant to be used for fun, or do they have a purpose?

SAY: If you're in a wheel chair, or you have to use crutches, it can be hard to pull or push a door open, so many companies have automatic doors, or doors with a button to help, or assist, people who might have trouble with the door on their own.

SAY: We all have things we need help with. Sometimes our parents, friends, or teachers can help us. Sometimes, it seems no one can, or no one is willing to help. But God wants us to know He is always available to help us. Sometimes He might ask us to do things that don't make a lot of sense, but if we trust Him and do what He says, we'll find out His ways really are best.

God And Me

GOD CAN TALK TO YOU AND ME!

SAY: Today we're going to read about three different people who asked for God's help and see how God assisted them. Last week we looked at a story about Daniel. This week we're going to look at another prayer Daniel prayed.

SAY: Daniel knew the people of Israel had sinned and that's why they lost the war and were taken as captives into Babylon. Daniel prayed and asked God to forgive them and help them escape Babylon. Let's read part of his prayer and find out what God did.

READ THE WORD
Have the kids follow along as the teacher or older kids read the following verses. **Daniel 9:4-8, 17-19**

SAY: First, Daniel tells God how Israel sinned. God already knew what they had done, but Daniel is admitting it. It's kind of like when your parents ask you about something you did even though they already know. Your parents want you to admit you did something wrong and take responsibility for your actions. Daniel was admitting to God that Israel had disobeyed God and he was asking God to forgive them. Then, Daniel asks God to rescue them from Babylon.

SAY: God sent an angel to Daniel with an answer. We won't look at the whole answer, just part of it.

READ THE WORD
Have the kids follow along as the teacher or older kids read the following verses. **Daniel 9:25**

ASK: Does that make any sense to you?

SAY: Probably not, but there are some things we can figure out. God had told another prophet, Jeremiah that Israel would be in captivity for seventy years before they returned to Israel. So the answer the angel gives Daniel, is explaining God's timing. He's not going to rescue Israel right away, but He is going to rescue them and gives Daniel some signs to look for so he knows when God is going to save Israel. But the angel says even more, he tells Daniel about Jesus. That's who the "Anointed One" is.

SAY: Daniel probably didn't understand everything God told him, but he trusted God and wrote down what God said so he would remember and be able to think about it, and watch for the signs. It gave Daniel hope while he was in a strange, and uncomfortable place.

Angela E. Powell

GOD CAN TALK TO YOU AND ME!

SAY: When we pray and ask God for help, we may not get the answer we're looking for, but God will always give us the answer we need. Another thing to remember is sometimes we go through hard times because we make bad choices. Sometimes God wants to make sure we learn not to make those bad decisions again. So He might ask us to wait a little longer before He helps us.

SAY: Other times, things happen to us that aren't fair. Let's read about Peter, who was put in jail because he was telling people about Jesus.

READ THE WORD
Have the kids follow along as the teacher or older kids read the following verses. **Acts 12:1-16**

SAY: Herod was killing Jesus' followers and now he had Peter! The church prayed for God to rescue Peter.

ASK: Do you think they believed God would really save Peter? Why or why not?

SAY: They were amazed to see him. Herod had already killed James, so it wasn't looking too good for Peter, but the church prayed anyway. They weren't expecting an angel to let Peter out of jail, but that's how God decided to save him. This is another example that God may not give us the answer we're looking for, but He always has the right answer.

SAY: We talked about God's instructions for how to pray and we talked about God providing for everything we need, but He may not give us everything we want.

ASK: Do you think we should pray for things we want as well as things we need?

SAY: We're going to read about a woman who wanted to have a son and see how God answered her prayer.

READ THE WORD
Have the kids follow along as the teacher or older kids read the following verses. **1 Samuel 1:6-11, 20**

SAY: God gave Hannah what she wanted, and to thank God, she did something amazing. She gave her son Samuel to the Lord. When he was about five years old, she took Samuel to the temple and left him there so he could grow up and learn how to serve the Lord.

God And Me

GOD CAN TALK TO YOU AND ME!

SAY: We don't have to do anything that extreme when God gives us what we want, but we should remember to thank him. God wants to give us the things we want, but sometimes the things we want, aren't good for us, and God isn't going to give us those things.

SAY: There are a lot of things we can ask God for, but we need to remember that asking God for things and for help is only part of prayer. We should remember the other parts as well.

HANDS-ON ACTIVITY

SUPPLIES: River stones, Colored sharpies, Mod Podge waterproof sealer, Foam paint brushes, Paper plates

- The stones should be rinsed and dried before class.
- Let each child choose a stone.
- Have them write "ASSIST" on the stone with the markers and let them decorate the stone.
- When they are done, let the kids paint a thin layer of mod podge over their stones.
- Let the stones dry on a paper plate with the child's name on it.
- Leave the stone in the classroom, the kids will take all 5 stones home at the end of the unit.

MEMORY VERSE

SAY: Let's say our memory verse a few times.

Matthew 6:9-13 – Our Father in heaven, may Your name be kept holy. May Your kingdom come soon. May Your will be done on earth, as it is in heaven. Give us today the food we need, and forgive us our sins as we have forgiven those who sin against us. And don't let us yield to temptation, but rescue us from the evil one.

PRAYER CIRCLES - Modified Sozo

As the children are learning to pray and hear God's voice, it can be helpful to give them each a notebook where they can write down what they're hearing and keep track of what they've been praying for. Keep these notebooks in class until you finish this curriculum. Encourage the kids to write down prayer requests they, or their peers have on the take home sheet so they can be reminded to pray for those things during the week.

SAY: Find a spot to sit where you can pray on your own and practice listening for God's voice. I want you to start by thinking of two things you can thank God for, write them down or draw a picture of them.

Give them about 2 minutes to do this.

GOD CAN TALK TO YOU AND ME!

SAY: Now, I want you to close your eyes and in your mind, ask God what He wants you to know about the lesson today. Ask Jesus what His favorite memory of you is, and ask Jesus to show you how He feels about you right now. Write down, or draw a picture of the first thing that comes to your mind for each question.

Give the kids 5 minutes unless they get restless and distracting. Encourage the kids to share with the class what they've heard from the past four weeks. It helps if you can take time during the week to pray about these questions yourself so you can share too.

God And Me

GOD CAN TALK TO YOU AND ME AT HOME!

LESSON SUMMARY: Today we talked about one of the easier aspects of prayer, asking God for what we need. We looked at Daniel, who asked God to forgive the people of Israel and rescue them from Babylon. Then we looked at Peter who was put in jail for telling people about Jesus. The church prayed for him and he was rescued in a way that surprised everyone. Finally, we looked at Hannah who prayed for a son when she was unable to have kids and God granted her request. We talked about the difference between needing something and wanting something and how God answers each type.

MEMORY VERSE: Matthew 6:9-13 – Our Father in heaven, may Your name be kept holy. May Your kingdom come soon. May Your will be done on earth, as it is in heaven. Give us today the food we need, and forgive us our sins as we have forgiven those who sin against us. And don't let us yield to temptation, but rescue us from the evil one.

IN THE CAR
Discuss the lesson with your kids. Some questions you could ask are:
- What is the difference between needing something and wanting something?
- How does God answer our prayers for things we need?
- How does God answer our prayers for things we want?
- Why would God not give us something we want?

AT MEALTIMES
- Read Psalm 30 together. David doesn't ask something in this Psalm, but he's thanking God for rescuing him. Discuss what David might have asked God based on what this Psalm says.
- Read Acts 12:1-18 together. Discuss why the church was surprised at Peter's rescue.

AT BEDTIME
Help your children learn to hear God's voice. Take five minutes and ask God something simple, then wait for His reply. It's good practice to write down what you hear so you can refer back to it. Some questions you could ask are:
- What was your favorite part about today?
- Where were you when I was doing _____?
- How do you feel about me right now?
- What do you want me to know about _____?

PRAYER REQUESTS:

Angela E. Powell

GOD CAN TALK TO YOU AND ME!

SUPPLIES NEEDED

Copies of take home sheet on page 179	River stones	Colored Sharpie markers
Mod Podge waterproof sealer	Foam paint brushes	Paper plates
Picture of a "Yield" street sign	Prayer notebooks	Pens or pencils
Paper		

LESSON 5: P.R.A.Y. YIELD
WELCOME

As you welcome children to class, have this question written on a white board, piece of paper, or ask the question to each child as you welcome them. Have the children find someone they don't know very well and discuss it.

Ice Breaker Question: What is the best piece of advice you've ever received?

GAME
PRAYER PLANES

SUPPLIES: Paper, Pens or pencils

- Give each child a piece of paper and have them write down a prayer request or praise.
- Once they've written down something to pray for, have them make a paper airplane from their paper.
- When everyone has a plane, have them stand in a line at one end of the room and throw their planes.
- Have them pick up a random plane, not their own if they can recognize them.
- Unfold the papers, and have each child pray for what is written on their piece of paper.

LESSON 5: P.R.A.Y. YIELD

Show the kids a picture of a "Yield" street sign.

ASK: Have you ever seen a sign like this? Do you know what it means? When you see a stop sign, do you always have to stop?

SAY: Yes! It doesn't matter if there are no cars coming down the road from any other direction, you have to stop. With a yield sign, you don't have to stop unless you can see other cars coming from other directions.

Draw a cross on a white board or paper to explain.

God And Me

GOD CAN TALK TO YOU AND ME!

SAY: If I have a yield sign, I have to stop for anyone crossing in front of me because they won't have a yield sign. The word "yield" means "to give way".

SAY: If some of you start having a conversation while I teach the lesson I'll ask you to stop. I can't make you stop, but I can ask you to yield to me or leave the room. That means you're giving up your conversation so I can teach. Now if you didn't yield to me and continued to talk, it would be really distracting because I wouldn't stop teaching just because you won't stop talking because when we're in here, it's my turn to talk unless I ask you a question.

SAY: If a car going one way, didn't yield to a car going another way, an accident could happen and people could be hurt. God gave us free will, which means we can choose to live our lives however we want, but God asks each of us to yield to His will. In other words, to put our wants and desires aside and do what God wants us to do.

SAY: Your parents want you to follow the rules at home because the rules keep you safe and teach you how to be responsible.

ASK: But if you don't yield to what they say, and you keep breaking the rules, what happens?

SAY: They might ground you, take your electronics away, or give you some other consequences. Those consequences are their way of saying, "It's important you yield to us. It's important you give up what you want to do and do what we want you to do." The reason they do that is because they know when you become an adult, if you don't yield to certain people, or to God, you could get into a lot of trouble.

SAY: God made each of us, so He knows what's best for us, even more than our parents do! And He is asking us to yield to Him and what He wants for us. For some people, this is easy. But for most of us, it can be really hard. We're going to look at some examples of people who yielded to God in the Bible.

SAY: First, we'll look at Jesus. He yielded to what God wanted because He knew God and trusted Him, but the thing God asked Him to do was very hard.

READ THE WORD
Have the kids follow along as the teacher or older kids read the following verses. **Luke 22:39-43**

GOD CAN TALK TO YOU AND ME!

SAY: Jesus knew God had sent Him to earth to die for the sins of every single person who ever lived or would ever live, including you and me. Jesus also knew when He would die and as the time got closer, Jesus started praying to see if maybe God had found another way to save people from sin, but Jesus didn't back out, He says, "Not my will, Lord, but Yours." He yielded to God's will even though He knew He would die a painful death.

SAY: Now let's look at someone else who yielded to God in a difficult situation. We're going to read about King Jehoshaphat. There were several surrounding countries that decided to go to war with Israel. When Jehoshaphat heard about it, he had everyone fast and pray. Fasting is when you don't eat anything for a certain period of time. Let's read what Jehoshaphat said in his prayer.

READ THE WORD
Have the kids follow along as the teacher or older kids read the following verses. **2 Chronicles 20:5-12**

SAY: We can see by his prayer that Israel had faced this enemy before and God let them live. Jehoshaphat could have decided that since they were God's chosen people, they could fight the enemy and win with no problem. Instead, he yielded to the Lord. He stopped his plans and waited to see what the Lord wanted to do. Let's find out how God answered.

READ THE WORD
Have the kids follow along as the teacher or older kids read the following verses. **2 Chronicles 20:15-18, 20-23**

SAY: In war, even though one side might win, people on both sides die. God decided He didn't want any of His people to die, so He fought the enemy of Israel on His own.

SAY: Jehoshaphat trusted God so much, he sent singers to the front of the army instead of fighters. And God had the enemies kill each other instead of the people of Israel.

SAY: If we are going to yield ourselves to God's will, we have to be able to trust God.

ASK: How do we do that? How do we learn to trust God?

God And Me

GOD CAN TALK TO YOU AND ME!

SAY: We learn to trust God by getting to know Him. The more time we spend getting to know God, the more we'll trust Him because He'll reveal more of Himself to us. We get to know Him through prayer and reading our Bibles. But if you just read your Bible, you'll learn what God did for other people. When we pray and get to know God through a personal relationship with Him, then you'll learn what God can do for you.

SAY: Remember to PRAY – Praise, Reveal, Assist, and Yield. Prayer is a two-way street. We can talk to God and God can talk to us. Let's practice hearing His voice more and more.

HANDS-ON ACTIVITY

SUPPLIES: River stones, Colored Sharpies, Mod Podge waterproof sealer, Foam paint brushes, Paper plates

- The stones should be rinsed and dried before class.
- Let each child choose a stone.
- Have them write "YIELD" on the stone with the markers and let them decorate the stone.
- When they are done, let the kids paint a thin layer of mod podge over their stones.
- Let the stones dry on a paper plate with the child's name on it.
- Let the kids take all five of their stones home.

MEMORY VERSE

SAY: Let's say our memory verse a few times.

Matthew 6:9-13 – Our Father in heaven, may Your name be kept holy. May Your kingdom come soon. May Your will be done on earth, as it is in heaven. Give us today the food we need, and forgive us our sins as we have forgiven those who sin against us. And don't let us yield to temptation, but rescue us from the evil one.

PRAYER CIRCLES - Modified Sozo

As the children are learning to pray and hear God's voice, it can be helpful to give them each a notebook where they can write down what they're hearing and keep track of what they've been praying for. Keep these notebooks in class until you finish this curriculum. Encourage the kids to write down prayer requests they, or their peers have on the take home sheet so they can be reminded to pray for those things during the week.

SAY: Find a spot to sit where you can pray on your own and practice listening for God's voice. I want you to start by thinking of two things you can thank God for, write them down or draw a picture of them.

GOD CAN TALK TO YOU AND ME!

Give them about 2 minutes to do this.

SAY: Now, I want you to close your eyes and in your mind, ask God what He wants you to know about yielding today. Also, ask God to show you what He's like. Ask Him if there is a lie you've been believing about Him. If He reveals something to you, ask God to replace the lie with His truth and show you what that truth is. Write down, or draw a picture of the first thing that comes to your mind for each question.

Give the kids 5 minutes unless they get restless and distracting. Encourage the kids to share with the class what they've heard from the past five weeks. It's helpful if you can spend time during the week praying about these questions yourself so you can share too.

God And Me

GOD CAN TALK TO YOU AND ME AT HOME!

LESSON SUMMARY: Today we discussed what the word "Yield" means. We used the example of a yield street sign, yielding to the rules of our parents and teachers, and then looked at two examples from the Bible. When Jesus prayed in the garden before His death and asked God if there was any other way to save people. But then He said, "Not my will, but Yours." We also looked at the story of Jehoshaphat. An enemy was coming against Israel and rumors were spreading that the enemy had been told by God to attack Israel. Instead of going out to fight, they yielded to the Lord and God fought for them.

MEMORY VERSE: Matthew 6:9-13 – Our Father in heaven, may Your name be kept holy. May Your kingdom come soon. May Your will be done on earth, as it is in heaven. Give us today the food we need, and forgive us our sins as we have forgiven those who sin against us. And don't let us yield to temptation, but rescue us from the evil one.

IN THE CAR
Discuss the lesson with your kids. Some questions you could ask are:
- What does "yield" mean?
- What do you think it means to yield to God?
- What is free will and why did God give it to us?

AT MEALTIMES
- Read Psalm 139 together. Discuss which parts show the four parts of prayer we've talked about over the past 5 weeks. Praise, Reveal, Assist, and Yield.
- Read verses 23-24 of Psalm 139 together. Discuss how David is yielding to God in these verses.

AT BEDTIME
Use the example of the Lord's Prayer and pray with your kids before they go to bed.
- Begin with Praise, or thanking the Lord.
- Ask Him to Reveal something to you about your day. This could be as simple as asking, "How were you with us today, Lord?" or "What do you want me to know about today?"
- Next, ask Him to Assist you and/or your children with something that's a struggle. This could be anything from helping a child to get up on time in the morning, to dealing with the loss of a family member.
- Finally, ask God to bring you all to a place where you want to yield to His will.

PRAYER REQUESTS:

© 2019 Angela E. Powell

Angela E. Powell

UNIT 6

UNIT THEME: GOD GAVE THE HOLY SPIRIT TO YOU AND ME

This lesson is a continuation on the subject of prayer, but identifies the role of the Holy Spirit in our lives as well. The children will learn that the Holy Spirit was sent to guide us through life and we can learn to hear His voice all the time, not just when we're in our times of prayer. Because this is such an important topic, the lessons are short in order to allow enough time for children to practice their prayer and listening to God skills.

Lesson 1: Who is the Holy Spirit?
This lesson introduces the Holy Spirit and why He was sent to us. The kids will learn how God is able to be a three-in-one being and how we can hear His voice. During prayer circle time the children will have more hands-on opportunities to build their prayer skills.

Lesson 2: The Holy Spirit is Like Fire
In this lesson the kids look at ways fire helps us and ways in which fire can be dangerous. Then we look at why the Bible describes the Holy Spirit like fire.

Lesson 3: The Holy Spirit is Like Wind
In this lesson the kids look at ways in which wind is good for us and ways in which wind can be dangerous. Then we look at why the Bible describes the Holy Spirit like wind.

Lesson 4: The Holy Spirit is like Water
In this lesson we look at ways in which water is good for us and ways in which it can be dangerous. Then we'll look at why the Bible describes the Holy Spirit like water.

Lesson 5: The Holy Spirit is Like a Dove
In this lesson we learn a little about doves and why the Bible says the Holy Spirit descended on Jesus like a dove.

Optional Videos For This Unit: https://bit.ly/2Ep4NXb

God And Me

GOD GAVE THE HOLY SPIRIT TO YOU AND ME!

SUPPLIES NEEDED

| Copies of take home sheet on page 186 | Balloons | Masking tape |
| Hardboiled egg | Prayer notebooks | Pens or pencils |

LESSON 1: WHO IS THE HOLY SPRIT?
WELCOME

As you welcome children to class, have this question written on a white board, piece of paper, or ask the question to each child as you welcome them. Have the children find someone they don't know very well and discuss it.

Ice Breaker Question: What makes a good life?

GAME
BALLOON RACE

SUPPLIES: Balloons, Masking tape

- Before class, put down two lines of masking tape, one on each end of the room.
- Have the kids line up on one side of the room on the line of masking tape.
- Give each child a balloon that hasn't been blown up. You may want to give each child a different colored balloon. If you have a lot of kids, you can divide into teams. The winner of each team can then compete in a final round.
- When you say "Go" have the kids blow up their balloons and release them, letting them fly across the room.
- When their balloon lands, they can run to it, fill it up again, and release it again. First one across the finish line wins.

LESSON 1: WHO IS THE HOLY SPIRIT?

Note: Understanding the Holy Spirit can be hard for many people to grasp, not just children. To help make the lesson clearer, you may want to consider reading the Bible passage from the Message Translation. That, and the New Living Translation were the versions used in creating this lesson.

ASK: Does anyone know where Jesus is living right now?

SAY: Jesus lives in heaven with God the Father, but He sent someone to live with us on earth.

ASK: Do you know who God sent to us?

Angela E. Powell

GOD GAVE THE HOLY SPIRIT TO YOU AND ME!

SAY: God sent the Holy Spirit!

ASK: Do you know who the Holy Spirit is?

SAY: God is a three part being. God the Father, God the Son, and God the Holy Spirit. We are also three part beings because God created us in His image.

ASK: Does anyone know how we are three part beings?

SAY: We have our body that everyone can see and touch. We have our minds and our emotions. Those can be seen by the expressions on our faces, they can also be heard when we speak. The third part of us is our spirit. That's the part of us that will live in heaven with Jesus if we have asked Him to be our Lord and Savior before we die.

HANDS-ON ACTIVITY

SUPPLIES: Hardboiled egg

Hold up the hardboiled egg.

SAY: To help you understand how God can be three beings in one, we're going to look at this hardboiled egg.

ASK: What is this outer part called? **(The shell!)** Is the shell a part of the egg? **(Yes!)**

Invite a child to come up and crack the shell and help you peel it.

ASK: We took off the shell, but is the shell still considered part of the egg?

SAY: Yes! It's still an egg shell even though it's no longer on the egg.

ASK: What is this next part of the egg called?

SAY: The egg white. It's the white part of the egg and it has lots of protein and good stuff in it for our bodies.

Invite another child to come and peel away the egg white.

SAY: Now we've taken the whole egg apart. It's in three different pieces. The shell, the egg white, and the yolk.

God And Me

GOD GAVE THE HOLY SPIRIT TO YOU AND ME!

Invite the kids to feel each part of the egg to see how each has a different texture.

ASK: When these three pieces are all together it's an egg, but is it still an egg if the pieces are divided like this?

SAY: Yes! We call each part by a new name, but it's still identified as an egg. Egg shell, egg white, and egg yolk. God the Father, God the Son, and God the Holy Spirit work the same way. They are all God, but they do different things. God the Father stays in heaven. He helped create the world and He wants us to look to Him as though He were a relative we're comfortable telling anything to.

SAY: God the Son is Jesus. He also helped create the earth, then came down and died for us so we could have a relationship with Him again. The Holy Spirit also helped create the earth, but let's read what Jesus says in the Bible about who the Holy Spirit is to find out more about Him.

READ THE WORD

Have the kids follow along as the teacher or older kids read the following verses. **John 14:15-27 (MSG or NLT version)**

SAY: This says the Holy Spirit is the Spirit of Truth. That's because we can learn to hear the voice of the Holy Spirit and when we do that, the Holy Spirit can tell us when we're believing a lie. He can tell us when we're doing something we shouldn't, and He can tell us which choices we should make.

SAY: For example, if you have a math test and an English test on the same day, the Holy Spirit can help you figure out how to study for both of them and which parts of your school books you should study.

ASK: But how do we hear the voice of the Holy Spirit?

SAY: The Holy Spirit talks to us through our thoughts. When we practice hearing God's voice we are actually hearing the Holy Spirit's voice. Sometimes it can be hard to tell if a thought came from us or from the Holy Spirit. That's why we need to read our Bibles and practice hearing His voice so we'll be able to tell whenever He talks to us. Because anything the Holy Spirit says to us, will line up with what the Bible says. The verses we read said we have to love Jesus if the Holy Spirit is going to come live inside of us.

ASK: How do we love Jesus?

SAY: We obey his commands or rules.

Angela E. Powell

GOD GAVE THE HOLY SPIRIT TO YOU AND ME!

ASK: What are Jesus' rules?

SAY: Do not murder, don't be jealous over what other people have, don't worship anything or anyone except the Lord, etc. But in Matthew 22, Jesus tells His followers that the greatest commandment is to love the Lord with all your heart, soul, and mind. Then He says the next greatest commandment is to love your neighbor as yourself.

SAY: God wants us to love Him and all the people around us and the Holy Spirit will help us do just that. Another job of the Holy Spirit is to help us understand the Bible. So if you read something in the Bible and you don't understand what you're reading, you can ask the Holy Spirit to help you.

SAY: Over the next four weeks, we're going to get to know the Holy Spirit even more, and we're going to practice hearing his voice.

MEMORY VERSE

SAY: Let's say our memory verse a few times.

John 14:23 – Jesus replied, "All who love Me will do what I say. My Father will love them, and We will come and make our home in each of them."

PRAYER CIRCLES - Modified Sozo

As the children are learning to pray and hear God's voice, it can be helpful to give them each a notebook where they can write down what they're hearing and keep track of what they've been praying for. Keep these notebooks in class until you finish this curriculum. Encourage the kids to write down prayer requests they, or their peers have on the take home sheet so they can be reminded to pray for those things during the week.

SAY: Today we're going to practice quieting our minds and bodies so we'll be able to hear the Holy Spirit.
- Have everyone sit down in a place where they cannot touch the person on any side of them when their arms are stretched out.
- Have everyone be quiet, then practice taking deep breaths with their eyes closed.
- Have the kids imagine what God might look like and have them try to focus on that image for one minute.
- If they have trouble, or their minds wander, encourage them to keep going back to that picture of what God looks like.

GOD GAVE THE HOLY SPIRIT TO YOU AND ME!

- Remind them to keep taking deep breaths while they look at the image in their mind.
- When a minute is up, ask the kids how their bodies feel after that exercise.

SAY: Next week, we're going to do that exercise again, but at the end of it, we're going to ask the Holy Spirt a question and write down what He tells us.

- Have kids get into groups of three or four with at least one older child or leader in each group.
- Have the kids share their prayer requests with the others in their group.
- Encourage each child to pray for one of the prayer requests presented.
- If no one has prayer requests or there aren't enough for everyone to pray about, give them suggestions such as, praying for a good, safe week for everyone or God would bring in more kids.
- If some groups finish before others, encourage the children to write down the prayer requests they heard in their group and/or spend time trying to hear God's voice.

Angela E. Powell

GOD GAVE THE HOLY SPIRT TO YOU AND ME AT HOME!

LESSON SUMMARY: Today we talked about the Trinity and identified how God can be one God, but also three separate entities. We used a hardboiled egg as an example. Then we looked at the Bible to see what Jesus had to say about the Holy Spirit. We looked at John 14:15-27 which is Jesus telling about how He is going to have to leave his followers, but is going to send a Helper to them when He goes.

MEMORY VERSE: John 14:23 – Jesus replied, "All who love Me will do what I say. My Father will love them, and We will come and make our home in each of them."

IN THE CAR
Discuss the lesson with your kids. Some questions you could ask are:
- How did the lesson make you feel?
- What did you learn about the Holy Spirit?
- What did the hardboiled egg show you about God?

AT MEALTIMES
- Invite a friend over for dinner sometime this week. Have a competition to see who can make your guest smile the most, but don't tell your guest what you're doing.
- Talk about the Holy Spirit. See if you can come up with other foods that have three parts like an egg does. Which parts would represent God the Father, God the Son, and God the Holy Spirit?
- The NIV translation of John 14:16 uses the word "Advocate" to describe the Holy Spirit. Grab a dictionary and read the definition of "Advocate". Discuss how the Holy Spirit is an advocate for us.

AT BEDTIME
Help your children learn to hear God's voice. Take five minutes and ask God something simple, then wait for His reply. It's good practice to write down what you hear so you can refer back to it. Some questions you could ask are:
- What was your favorite part about today?
- Where were you when I was doing _____?
- How do you feel about me right now?
- What do you want me to know about _____?
- Show me a happy time from my past when you were with me.

PRAYER REQUESTS:

God And Me

GOD SENT THE HOLY SPIRIT TO YOU AND ME!

SUPPLIES NEEDED

Copies of take home sheet on page 191	Slime making supplies (*) Blindfolds
Masking tape Cups	*Bowls *Washable school glue
*Glitter and/or food coloring (optional)	*Disposable spoons or sticks
*Borax powder, liquid starch, or saline solution	*Measuring cups and spoons
Prayer notebooks	Pens or pencils

LESSON 2: THE HOLY SPIRIT IS LIKE FIRE
WELCOME

As you welcome children to class, have this question written on a white board, piece of paper, or ask the question to each child as you welcome them. Have the children find someone they don't know very well and discuss it.

Ice Breaker Question: What is the last adventure you went on?

GAME
TRUSTING GOD IN THE MINEFIELD

SUPPLIES: Cups, Blindfolds, Masking tape

- Before class, make a large square on the floor with masking tape. This will be the minefield.
- Set up cups randomly in the minefield. These are the mines.
- If you have a lot of kids, you may want to make several squares and have teams compete.
- Divide kids into pairs. The one who wears the blindfold will walk through the minefield.
- When you say "Go" the child not wearing a blindfold will attempt to direct the blindfolded child through the minefield. If the child with the blindfold runs into any of the cups, the game is over.
- Children from other teams can try to distract the children going through the minefield with talking or yelling so the blindfolded child has a harder time hearing their teammate, but they can't call out directions to make them run into cups.
- You can use this example to show how the Holy Spirit can guide us through life.

LESSON 2: THE HOLY SPIRIT IS LIKE FIRE

ASK: Can anyone tell me who the three persons of God are?

SAY: God the Father, Jesus, and the Holy Spirit.

ASK: Does anyone remember why Jesus sent the Holy Spirit to us?

Angela E. Powell

GOD SENT THE HOLY SPIRIT TO YOU AND ME!

SAY: He's our helper and the Spirit of Truth. He helps us understand the Bible, do the right things, and helps us when we have choices to make.

SAY: Last week we read about when Jesus told his followers He would send them the Holy Spirit after He left the earth and went back to heaven. Today we're going to read about the day of Pentecost, which is the day the Holy Spirit came to live inside the followers of Jesus and how the Holy Spirit can now live inside everyone who believes Jesus is their Savior. Let's read what happened.

READ THE WORD
Have the kids follow along as the teacher or older kids read the following verses. **Acts 2:1-12**

HANDS-ON ACTIVITY
SLIME
SUPPLIES: Bowls, Spoons or sticks, School glue, Measuring cups & spoons, Borax powder, liquid starch, or saline solution, Fun mix in's such as glitter and food coloring (optional)

NOTE: There are hundreds of slime recipes online. Feel free to use your favorite.
SIMPLE SLIME RECIPE[7]
- 1/2 cup of Clear or White Washable PVA School Glue
- 1/4-1/2 cup of Liquid Starch
- 1/2 cup of Water
- Food Coloring, Glitter, Confetti, and other Fun Mix-Ins

1. Measure and pour glue into a bowl.
2. Add water and mix to combine.
3. Add food coloring and other add-ins if using. Mix well.
4. Measure the liquid starch and add to the bowl. Mix until slime forms.

SAY: When we accept Jesus as our Lord and Savior, the Holy Spirit begins living inside us. It might be hard to believe because we can't see Him. Let's try an experiment to help us understand.

- Divide the kids into groups of four.
- Let each group make their slime and divide it between the members of their group.
- Invite the kids to pray and ask the Holy Spirit to give them an image of what He's like. Then have the kids use the slime to create it.

---

[7] https://littlebinsforlittlehands.com/simple-slime-recipe-that-actually-works/

God And Me

GOD SENT THE HOLY SPIRIT TO YOU AND ME!

ASK: Can any of you see the glue you poured into your slime? What about the water? The borax powder? Why can't you see the individual ingredients? How are the slime ingredients like or unlike how the Holy Spirit lives in us?

SAY: The separate ingredients aren't visible anymore, but they're still there. They just look different. The same is true when we ask Jesus to be our Lord and Savior. The Holy Spirit is inside us and because of that we will never be the same. We'll start to look different as the Holy Sprit works in our lives.

SAY: Our Bible verses said the disciples saw what looked like tongues of fire resting on each of them. The Holy Spirit is said to be like fire.

ASK: What do you think that means? How is fire useful?

SAY: It gives us heat, light, and a way to cook food.

ASK: How is fire dangerous?

SAY: It can burn us, it can cause a lot of destruction if it gets out of control.

SAY: So we could say the Holy Spirit has power and energy like fire does. The Holy Spirit won't burn us though. He'll burn up any sin we have in our lives if we let Him, or He might put a burning desire in us to pray for someone or help someone.

ASK: What do you think it means to have a burning desire?

SAY: It means you're so passionate about something you *have* to do that thing. It's kind of like when you have some money and someone says that money is burning a hole in your pocket. What they're saying is you can't stop thinking about what you're going to spend that money on and you keep asking when you can go to the store.

SAY: Let's review. The Holy Spirit is like fire.

ASK: What are two things the Holy Spirit will do in us that makes us think of fire?

SAY: He'll burn up sin. He'll make us passionate for the things He wants us to do. Next week we're going to look at how the Holy Spirit is like wind.

GOD SENT THE HOLY SPIRIT TO YOU AND ME!

MEMORY VERSE
SAY: Let's say our memory verse a few times.

John 14:23 – Jesus replied, "All who love Me will do what I say. My Father will love them, and We will come and make our home in each of them."

PRAYER CIRCLES - Modified Sozo
As the children are learning to pray and hear God's voice, it can be helpful to give them each a notebook where they can write down what they're hearing and keep track of what they've been praying for. Keep these notebooks in class until you finish this curriculum. Encourage the kids to write down prayer requests they, or their peers have on the take home sheet so they can be reminded to pray for those things during the week.

- Hand out the prayer notebooks to each child. Explain that they are only to pick the notebook up when they are ready to start writing down what the Holy Spirit is telling them.
- Have everyone sit down in a place where they cannot touch the person on any side of them when their arms are stretched out.
- Have everyone be quiet, then practice taking deep breaths with their eyes closed.
- Have the kids imagine what God might look like and have them try to focus on that image.
- If they have trouble, or their minds wander, encourage them to keep going back to that picture of what God looks like.
- Remind them to keep taking deep breaths while they look at the image in their mind.
- When everyone looks calm and relaxed, have them ask the Holy Spirit the following: Holy Spirit, in what way are you like fire in my life? Holy Spirit show me a picture of what you are like. Holy Spirit ow do you feel about me right now?
- Encourage the kids to write down, or draw a picture of the first thing that comes to their mind. Give them about five minutes to do this.
- If anyone wants to share, give them time to do so.

God And Me

GOD SENT THE HOLY SPIRIT TO YOU AND ME AT HOME!

LESSON SUMMARY: Today we looked at how the Holy Spirit is like fire. We read about the day of Pentecost when the followers of Jesus were baptized in the Holy Spirit and spoke in other tongues. We looked at the characteristics of fire and compared those to the Holy Spirit. Fire can be both good for us, and dangerous. We talked about how God can put pressure, or heat, on us when we have sin in our lives we aren't ready to give up. The kids also practiced hearing the voice of the Holy Spirit and writing down what they heard Him say.

MEMORY VERSE: John 14:23 – Jesus replied, "All who love Me will do what I say. My Father will love them, and We will come and make our home in each of them."

IN THE CAR
Discuss the lesson with your kids. Some questions you could ask are:
- How did the lesson make you feel?
- What did you learn about the Holy Spirit?
- How is the Holy Spirit like fire?

AT MEALTIMES
- Talk about the dangers of fire, then discuss in what ways God is powerful like fire. See if you can find examples in the Bible.
- Talk about how fire can be good, then discuss in what ways God is like those examples. See if you can find examples in the Bible.
- Make a list of God's characteristics, then think of earthly things you could compare those characteristics to.

AT BEDTIME
Help your children learn to hear God's voice. Take five minutes and ask God something simple, then wait for His reply. It's good practice to write down what you hear so you can refer back to it. Some questions you could ask are:
- What was your favorite part about today?
- Where were you when I was doing _____?
- How do you feel about me right now?
- What do you want me to know about _____?
- Show me a happy time from my past when you were with me.

PRAYER REQUESTS:

© 2019 Angela E. Powell

Angela E. Powell

GOD SENT THE HOLY SPIRIT TO YOU AND ME!

SUPPLIES NEEDED

- Copies of take home sheet on page 196
- Craft sticks
- Dish soap
- Pens or pencils
- 1 Tall, narrow plastic bottle OR 2 soda bottles
- Building blocks
- Duct tape or Tornado tube
- Food coloring
- Tornado facts video
- Index cards
- Water
- Prayer notebooks

LESSON 3: THE HOLY SPIRIT IS LIKE WIND

WELCOME

As you welcome children to class, have this question written on a white board, piece of paper, or ask the question to each child as you welcome them. Have the children find someone they don't know very well and discuss it.

Ice Breaker Question: What is the most memorable gift you've received?

GAME

WIND POWERED CAR RACE

SUPPLIES: Legos, Index cards, Craft sticks, Tape

- If you have the budget you can buy the small Lego car kits. You can also ask parents if you can borrow their Legos, but make sure you get enough wheels so all the kids will have enough.
- Give the kids five minutes to build a Lego car. Explain that it must have wheels.
- Once their car is built, have them tape one end of a craft stick to an index card and the other end to their car.
- If you have a lot of kids, you may want to do this in groups. As soon as a certain number of children finish their cars, have them race. Continue making groups as kids finish their cars.
- Have the kids line up and blow on the index card on their car to make the car move. Have them blow three or four times then see who got their car the farthest.
- Let all the kids have one turn to race.
- If the kids have raced, they can make adjustments to their car and race with others again until all the kids have had a chance to go at least once.
- Don't play for more than fifteen minutes.
- Alternately, you could use matchbox cars, let the kids cut and create a 'sail' for their car and tape it on and then race the cars.

God And Me

GOD SENT THE HOLY SPIRIT TO YOU AND ME!

LESSON 3: THE HOLY SPIRIT IS LIKE WIND

ASK: Have you ever experienced a really strong wind?

SAY: When wind gets moving really fast, it can cause trees to fall down.

ASK: What type of storm do you think makes the fastest wind?

SAY: Tornadoes can make wind go as fast as 300 miles per hour. That's some pretty fast wind!

Show a video about tornado facts and/or talk about the following facts: [8]
NOTE: There is a link on the overview page where you can find videos for this unit or you can use your own.

- Tornadoes are columns of fast spinning air.
- Tornadoes are formed when cold, dry air moving in one direction, bumps into warm, wet air coming from a different direction. The two types of wind force each other to start spinning.
- Tornadoes sound like a loud speeding train, but they move pretty slowly.

SAY: Today we're going to look at how the Holy Spirit is like wind. Let's see what the Bible has to say about this.

READ THE WORD

Have the kids follow along as the teacher or older kids read the following verses. **Acts 2:1-2, John 20:22**

SAY: Just like we saw with the fire, the Holy Spirit has so much power it's like being in a strong wind storm, but the Holy Spirit can also be gentle like a breath. When it's hot outside it can feel really good when the wind starts to blow a little bit.

ASK: Can anyone show me what that feels like? It's refreshing and makes us smile, right?

SAY: When we learn to hear the voice of the Holy Spirit and we let Him guide us and help us, it makes us feel refreshed and happy.

---

[8] Tornado speed reference: https://abcnews.go.com/Technology/Weather/story?id=99457&page=1

Angela E. Powell

GOD SENT THE HOLY SPIRIT TO YOU AND ME!

HANDS-ON ACTIVITY (OPTIONAL)

SUPPLIES: Tall narrow plastic bottle OR 2 large soda bottles with a tornado tube, Water, Dish soap, Food coloring

- Show the kids the bottle(s) and explain that we're going to make a tornado.
- Fill up one water bottle to the top with water.
- Add a couple drops of dish soap. You can also add food coloring for added effect.
- Close the bottle, or add the tornado tube and attach the second bottle.
- Shake and swirl the bottle. If using two bottles, swirl and tip upside down.
- Watch the tornado.
- Let the kids spend a few minutes taking turns trying to create the tornado themselves.

SAY: This week I want you to practice hearing the voice of the Holy Spirit and see if you can come up with more wind examples to describe the Holy Spirit.

MEMORY VERSE

SAY: Let's say our memory verse a few times.

John 14:23 – Jesus replied, "All who love Me will do what I say. My Father will love them, and We will come and make our home in each of them."

PRAYER CIRCLES - Modified Sozo

As the children are learning to pray and hear God's voice, it can be helpful to give them each a notebook where they can write down what they're hearing and keep track of what they've been praying for. Keep these notebooks in class until you finish this curriculum. Encourage the kids to write down prayer requests they, or their peers have on the take home sheet so they can be reminded to pray for those things during the week.

- Hand out the children's prayer notebooks and pen's or pencils. Tell the kids they're only to pick the notebook up when they are ready to start writing what the Holy Spirit is telling them.
- Have everyone sit down where they can't touch the person on any side of them when their arms are stretched out.
- Have everyone be quiet, then practice taking deep breaths with their eyes closed.
- Have the kids imagine what God might look like and have them try to focus on that image.
- If they have trouble focusing, encourage them to go back to the image of what God looks like.
- Remind them to take deep breaths while they look at the image in their mind.

GOD SENT THE HOLY SPIRIT TO YOU AND ME!

- When everyone looks calm, have them ask the Holy Spirit the following: Holy Spirit, what do you want me to know about you today? What is your favorite memory of me? What is something I should know about you?
- Encourage the kids to write down, or draw a picture of the first thing that comes to their mind. Give them about five minutes to do this.
- If anyone wants to share, let them.

Angela E. Powell

GOD SENT THE HOLY SPIRIT TO YOU AND ME AT HOME!

LESSON SUMMARY: Today we looked at how the Holy Spirit is like wind. We looked at verses of how the Holy Spirit is like a strong wind and a gentle breath. Then we looked at tornadoes and learned how they're formed and how fast the wind can blow in a tornado. We also spent time practicing how to hear the voice of the Holy Spirit and writing down what He told us.

MEMORY VERSE: John 14:23 – Jesus replied, "All who love Me will do what I say. My Father will love them, and We will come and make our home in each of them."

IN THE CAR
Discuss the lesson with your kids. Some questions you could ask are:
- What did you learn about the Holy Spirit?
- How is the Holy Spirit like wind?
- What did you learn about tornados?

AT MEALTIMES
- Talk about the dangers of strong wind, then discuss in what ways God is powerful like wind. See if you can find examples in the Bible.
- Talk about how wind can be good, then discuss in what ways God is like those examples. See if you can find examples in the Bible.
- Make a list of God's characteristics, then think of earthly things you could compare those characteristics to.

AT BEDTIME
Help your children learn to hear God's voice. Take five minutes and ask God something simple, then wait for His reply. It's good practice to write down what you hear so you can refer back to it. Some questions you could ask are:
- What was your favorite part about today?
- Where were you when I was doing _____?
- How do you feel about me right now?
- What do you want me to know about _____?
- Show me a happy time from my past when you were with me.

PRAYER REQUESTS:

God And Me

GOD SENT THE HOLY SPIRIT TO YOU AND ME!

SUPPLIES NEEDED
Copies of take home sheet on page 201	Water	Straws	Wax paper
Spoon or Eyedropper	Tape	Towel	Pens or pencils
Prayer notebooks	Kids knocked over by waves video		

LESSON 4: THE HOLY SPIRIT IS LIKE WATER

WELCOME

As you welcome children to class, have this question written on a white board, piece of paper, or ask the question to each child as you welcome them. Have the children find someone they don't know very well and discuss it.

Ice Breaker Question: What do you like most about your family?

GAME

WATER DROPLET RACE

SUPPLIES: Water, Straws, Wax paper, Spoon or eye dropper, Tape, Towel

- Before class, cover the top of a small table with wax paper and tape it down.
- Give each child a straw and have them line up in two lines on the short side of the table.
- Using the spoon or eye dropper, make two nickel sized water drops on the wax paper near the kids.
- When you say "Go", the first two kids in line will start blowing through their straw to move the water across the table until it falls off on the opposite end.
- If the water falls off the sides of the table, add another drop near where the drop fell off the table and let the child continue.
- You can have a towel on the floor under the table, or at the end of the table to catch the water that falls off.
- When one child has finished, they will run to the back of their line and the next child in line will begin the race.
- The first team to finish one round wins.
- If you have a lot of kids, you can have multiple tables. For added fun, once each table has a winner, you can have the winning teams compete against each other until one team becomes the ultimate winner.

Angela E. Powell

GOD SENT THE HOLY SPIRIT TO YOU AND ME!

LESSON 4: THE HOLY SPIRIT IS LIKE WATER

ASK: Have any of you ever gone swimming in the ocean or in a wave pool? If so, what was it like? Did you get knocked over by a wave or get pulled off your feet as the water rushed back from the shore?

NOTE: If not many kids have experienced the power of water, there are videos online you can show of kids getting knocked down by waves. There is a link on the overview page where you can find videos for this unit or you can use your own.

SAY: So far we've looked at how the Holy Spirit is like wind and fire. Both can be powerful and dangerous, but both can also be good and helpful.

ASK: In what ways are fire and wind helpful?

SAY: Fire provides heat and helps us cook our food. Wind can help us cool down on a really hot day.

ASK: Does anyone remember how fire and wind remind us of the Holy Spirit?

SAY: The Holy Spirit is like fire because He burns up sin in our lives or makes life uncomfortable for us if we don't give up sinning, just like sitting next to a fire for too long can become uncomfortable. He can also make us passionate for certain things He wants us to do. He's like the wind because He can refresh us. When we learn to listen for His voice and let Him guide us and help us then life will feel easier, we'll feel lighter and happier.

ASK: So how do you think the Holy Spirit is like water? What can we do with water?

SAY: Take a shower and get clean, go swimming, hydrate our bodies, it makes plants grow, etc. Let's read what the Bible has to say about the Holy Spirit being like water.

READ THE WORD

Have the kids follow along as the teacher or older kids read the following verses. **John 7:37-39, John 4:14, 1 Corinthians 12:13**

SAY: There are a lot of good things we get from water. It's cleansing and healthy for our bodies. In the same way, the Holy Spirit cleanses us. Just like fire can burn up dead stuff, and the Holy Spirit can burn away sin when we're ready to give it up, the Holy Spirit can also wash us from sin. When we ask God to forgive us of sin, the Holy Spirit washes that sin away like it was never there.

GOD SENT THE HOLY SPIRIT TO YOU AND ME!

ASK: How many of you have ever had a cold glass of water after playing outside on a hot day? It's good, right?

SAY: It tastes good, it feels good because it cools us down and our bodies love it because it's restoring the water our bodies lost while we were playing. We read a couple of verses that talked about being thirsty.

SAY: We can be thirsty for more than just water. We can be thirsty for friendships, knowledge, food, and happiness. It's good to be happy. We all like being happy, but when we look at our friends and family to bring us happiness, or our favorite video game, or favorite dessert, those will only make us happy for a short time.

SAY: It's like getting a glass of water. Eventually, you're going to have to go and get more water because one glass won't last you your whole life. If we're looking for happiness in video games, we're eventually going to realize they don't really make us happy.

SAY: The Holy Spirit is like a fountain of water we have with us all the time and can drink from all the time. He is our true source of happiness and when we learn to include Him in our lives every day, we'll find we aren't as thirsty for people and things because God is filling us up and quenching our thirst.

SAY: This week, whenever you get a drink of water, juice, soda, or anything, I want you to think about how God quenches our thirst.

MEMORY VERSE
SAY: Let's say our memory verse a few times.

John 14:23 – Jesus replied, "All who love Me will do what I say. My Father will love them, and We will come and make our home in each of them."

PRAYER CIRCLES - Modified Sozo
As the children are learning to pray and hear God's voice, it can be helpful to give them each a notebook where they can write down what they're hearing and keep track of what they've been praying for. Keep these notebooks in class until you finish this curriculum. Encourage the kids to write down prayer requests they, or their peers have on the take home sheet so they can be reminded to pray for those things during the week.

Angela E. Powell

GOD SENT THE HOLY SPIRIT TO YOU AND ME!

- Hand out the children's prayer notebooks and pen's or pencils. Explain that they are only to pick the notebook up when they are ready to start writing down what the Holy Spirit is telling them.
- Have everyone sit down in a place where they cannot touch the person on any side of them when their arms are stretched out.
- Have everyone be quiet, then practice taking deep breaths with their eyes closed.
- Have the kids imagine what God might look like and have them try to focus on that image.
- If they have trouble, or their minds wander, encourage them to keep going back to that picture of what God looks like.
- Remind them to keep taking deep breaths while they look at the image in their mind.
- When everyone looks calm and relaxed, have them ask the Holy Spirit the following: Holy Spirit, show me a happy memory from my past where you were with me.
- Have them spend a few minutes exploring that memory with God. They can ask Jesus where He was in that memory and what His favorite part of that memory was.
- Encourage the kids to write down, or draw a picture of the first thing that comes to their mind. Give them about ten minutes to do this.
- If anyone wants to share, give them time to do so.

God And Me

GOD SENT THE HOLY SPIRIT TO YOU AND ME AT HOME!

LESSON SUMMARY: Today we looked at how the Holy Spirit is like water. We looked at verses that show examples of how the Holy Spirit is like water. We also spent time practicing how to hear the voice of the Holy Spirit and writing down what He told us.

MEMORY VERSE: John 14:23 – Jesus replied, "All who love Me will do what I say. My Father will love them, and We will come and make our home in each of them."

IN THE CAR
Discuss the lesson with your kids. Some questions you could ask are:
- What did you learn about the Holy Spirit?
- How is the Holy Spirit like water?
- What did the Holy Spirit tell you today?

AT MEALTIMES
- Talk about the power of water, then discuss in what ways God is powerful. See if you can find examples in the Bible.
- Talk about how water can be good, then discuss in what ways God is like those examples. See if you can find examples in the Bible.
- Make a list of God's characteristics, then think of earthly things you could compare those characteristics to.

AT BEDTIME
Help your children learn to hear God's voice. Take five minutes and ask God something simple, then wait for His reply. It's good practice to write down what you hear so you can refer back to it. Some questions you could ask are:
- What was your favorite part about today?
- Where were you when I was doing _____?
- How do you feel about me right now?
- What do you want me to know about _____?
- Show me a happy time from my past when you were with me.

PRAYER REQUESTS:

© 2019 Angela E. Powell

Angela E. Powell

GOD SENT THE HOLY SPIRIT TO YOU AND ME!

SUPPLIES NEEDED

Copies of take home sheet on page 206   Prayer notebooks   Pens or pencils
Dove facts video   Holy Spirit landing on Jesus like a dove video

LESSON 5: THE HOLY SPIRIT IS LIKE A DOVE

WELCOME

As you welcome children to class, have this question written on a white board, piece of paper, or ask the question to each child as you welcome them. Have the children find someone they don't know very well and discuss it.

Ice Breaker Question: What are three interesting facts about you?

GAME
THE SILENT GAME

SUPPLIES: None

- Divide kids into groups of three.
- Each group is going to try and knock the other children out of their group. The way they do this is by staying silent the longest.
- Children can try to make each other laugh, but if they make themselves laugh in the process they're out.
- Once there is one winner from each group, have those children sit in a circle facing each other. They will continue the process of trying to make each other laugh or speak.
- The children who were knocked out, can form a circle around them and try to get them to laugh or speak as well by asking questions, or calling their name, but they are not allowed to touch any of the children or say mean things. They must also keep the volume low enough so you can tell if anyone in the middle circle makes a noise.
- Coughing or sneezing do not count as making noise.
- The last child to keep silent is the winner.
- If the game goes over the time, announce that the remaining kids won the game.

LESSON 5: THE HOLY SPIRIT IS LIKE A DOVE

SAY: We've compared the Holy Spirit to fire, water, and wind.

ASK: Does anyone remember how the Holy Spirit is like these things?

God And Me

GOD SENT THE HOLY SPIRIT TO YOU AND ME!

SAY: The Holy Spirit is like fire because He can make us feel uncomfortable if we aren't ready to give up a sin He wants us to, just like it's uncomfortable to sit next to a fire for too long. He refreshes us and washes away our sin, just like a cold glass of water on a hot day is refreshing. Water is also used to wash our clothes and bodies. The Holy Spirit is like a powerful wind storm and a gentle breath. A cool breeze on a hot day feels good and spending time with the Holy Spirit makes us feel good too.

SAY: Today we're going to look at how the Holy Spirit is like a dove.

ASK: When you think of a dove, what comes to mind?

SAY: Those are great answers! We might think of the color white, or soft, or cute.

ASK: Does anyone know what kind of personality a dove has?

NOTE: You can watch a video about dove facts, or explain that doves are gentle, domesticated, calm, relaxed, and they love people. There is a link on the overview page where you can find videos for this unit or you can use your own.

ASK: They sound like really nice birds don't they?

SAY: Before we compare doves to the Holy Spirit, let's see what the Bible says about the Holy Spirit being like a dove.

READ THE WORD

Have the kids follow along as the teacher or older kids read the following verses. **Matthew 3:16, Mark 1:10, Luke 3:22, John 1:32**

NOTE: You can watch a video that shows a good example of the Holy Spirit descending on Jesus like a dove. There is a link on the overview page where you can find videos for this unit or you can use your own.

SAY: The Bible doesn't say much about the Holy Spirit being like a dove, but it's one of the most used symbols to describe the Holy Spirit.

ASK: Why do you think that is?

SAY: Those are great answers! Let's look at some verses in the Bible that tell us how we will act if we have the Holy Spirit in our lives and talk to Him on a regular basis.

Angela E. Powell

GOD SENT THE HOLY SPIRIT TO YOU AND ME!

READ THE WORD
Have the kids follow along as the teacher or older kids read the following verses. **Galatians 5:22-23**

ASK: Which of these things remind you of the dove facts we spoke about earlier? Most of these could work couldn't they?

SAY: Doves are calm and don't get nervous easily. You could say they are peaceful, gentle, and patient with humans! They love people. Love is one description of the Holy Spirit, but you could also say they're faithful to humans. They stick around and don't fly off. They're also faithful to other doves. They're kind because they don't bite. The Holy Spirit is the same. He loves us, He's faithful to stay with us and help us. He's patient, kind, and gentle. He's also joyful.

SAY: There is a lot to know about the Holy Spirit but the only way to really understand who the Holy Spirit is, is to spend time with Him. The more time you spend with the Holy Spirit the better you'll know Him. It's the same when we make friends. We aren't automatically friends with people. We have to get to know them first.

SAY: Just because we're going to move on to a new topic next week doesn't mean you should stop listening to the Holy Spirit. I hope you'll all keep practicing with your families and writing down what you hear.

MEMORY VERSE
SAY: Let's say our memory verse a few times.

John 14:23 – Jesus replied, "All who love Me will do what I say. My Father will love them, and We will come and make our home in each of them."

PRAYER CIRCLES - Modified Sozo
As the children are learning to pray and hear God's voice, it can be helpful to give them each a notebook where they can write down what they're hearing and keep track of what they've been praying for. Keep these notebooks in class until you finish this curriculum. Encourage the kids to write down prayer requests they, or their peers have on the take home sheet so they can be reminded to pray for those things during the week.
- Hand out the children's prayer notebooks and pen's or pencils. Explain that they are only to pick the notebook up when they are ready to start writing down what the Holy Spirit is telling them.
- Have everyone sit down in a place where they cannot touch the person on any side of them when their arms are stretched out.

GOD SENT THE HOLY SPIRIT TO YOU AND ME!

- Have everyone be quiet, then practice taking deep breaths with their eyes closed.
- Have the kids imagine what God might look like and have them try to focus on that image.
- If they have trouble, or their minds wander, encourage them to keep going back to that picture of what God looks like.
- Remind them to keep taking deep breaths while they look at the image in their mind.
- When everyone looks calm and relaxed, have them ask the Holy Spirit the following: Holy Spirit what do you want me to know about the lesson today? What do you want me to know about you that I don't know already? Show me ways I can stay connected with you. Please remind me to spend time with you everyday.
- Encourage the kids to write down, or draw a picture of the first thing that comes to their mind. Give them about five minutes to do this.
- If anyone wants to share, give them time to do so.
- Let the children take their notebooks home today.

Angela E. Powell

GOD SENT THE HOLY SPIRIT TO YOU AND ME AT HOME!

LESSON SUMMARY: Today we looked at how the Holy Spirit is like a dove. We looked at verses that show examples of how the Holy Spirit is like a dove and looked at dove facts. We also spent some time practicing how to hear the voice of the Holy Spirit and writing down what He told us.

MEMORY VERSE: John 14:23 – Jesus replied, "All who love Me will do what I say. My Father will love them, and We will come and make our home in each of them."

IN THE CAR
Discuss the lesson with your kids. Some questions you could ask are:
- What did you learn about the Holy Spirit?
- How is the Holy Spirit like a dove?
- What did the Holy Spirit tell you today?

AT MEALTIMES
- Read Galatians 5:22-23 with your family. Talk about the characteristics of the Holy Spirit. Discuss which of those characteristics each of your family members have and which ones need practice.
- Based on Galatians 5:22-23, we are supposed to produce the fruits of the spirit. Discuss how we learn to produce the characteristics listed in these verses.
- Think about the fruits of the spirit. What other animals can you think of that show these characteristics other than a dove?

AT BEDTIME
Help your children learn to hear God's voice. Take five minutes and ask God something simple, then wait for His reply. It's good practice to write down what you hear so you can refer back to it. Some questions you could ask are:
- What was your favorite part about today?
- Where were you when I was doing _____?
- How do you feel about me right now?
- What do you want me to know about _____?
- Show me a happy time from my past when you were with me.

PRAYER REQUESTS:

REFERENCE

If you have questions or comments about this curriculum feel free to contact me at authoraepowell@gmail.com or drop me note on my website at www.angelaepowell.com.

Information on the three prayer methods used in this book

"God With Me" Prayer - The Prayer Circles that invite the children to participate in Interactive Gratitude and write their prayers as though they were having a face to face conversation with God, come from the book "Joyful Journey: Listening To Immanuel" by E. James Wilder, Anna Kang, John Loppnow, and Sungshim Loppnow.

This method of learning to hear God's voice comes from discoveries in brain science that reveal God created our brains for relationship. Our brains seek to find people who are glad to be with us and there are several ways our brains figure out who is glad to be with us, and who is not. One of these is ways is through attunement (Someone who can meet me in my pain in a safe, compassionate, and kind way).

We all have times when we aren't glad to be with someone and it's been discovered that thinking about things we appreciate, especially times we've appreciated a person, can restore our brain's desire to connect with people again. There are many reasons our brains shut down and don't want to connect with other people, but these dim relational circuits can also cause us to have a difficult time hearing from God.

The "God With Me" Prayer method begins with Interactive Gratitude to make sure our brains are fully online and wanting to connect with other people and with God. The gratitude exercise is more than just remembering something or someone you're thankful for. The goal is to immerse yourself in the memory until you feel the appreciation again. When inviting the kids into this part of the prayer time, they can think of friends and family who they appreciate, but as they begin to have better success hearing God's voice, encourage them to consider times when they felt gratitude toward God as they spent time with Him.

They can also keep a list of these memories in their notebooks. The best way to do this is to give each of the gratitude memories a short title that reminds them of the whole memory when they look it over again. This will make the process faster each time as they won't have to think up a new memory each time. However, be aware, these gratitude memories can lose their effectiveness if used too often. The kids should try to come up with a new memory every couple of times they try this method.

After Interactive Gratitude, the kids will think of things they can pray about. It might be easier to start with simple things as they first begin. This method is very effective in dealing with emotionally traumatic events, but if those events are triggered in a child, and they aren't hearing God's voice confidently, they may find themselves stuck in that negative experience. However, it's not always easy to determine when a child will choose a topic that could trigger these deep emotional reactions because anything can cause our brain emotional trauma (pain that is not processed in a safe and healthy way). That means something as simple as not being invited to play in a game on the school playground could cause emotional trauma.

If a child gets upset, starts acting out unreasonably, or simply cries, make sure to check in with them. If it seems they're struggling to hear God's voice on the matter they've chosen to pray about, have them go back to the Interactive Gratitude until they can feel that appreciation again. Don't let them return to the prayer on their own. If you can't sit and guide them through the process of hearing the Lord, then have them stay on Interactive Gratitude. This usually means their capacity for joy is low and the Interactive Gratitude will help them grow their capacity. Once they've gotten good at being able to recall memories of gratitude, have them try the rest of the process again, but maybe with a different topic.

The next part of this prayer method invites the kids to talk to God about what's on their hearts and allow Him to attune to them. The kids write down their prayer, then write down what God might say in response to that prayer in the following order:
"I see you."
"I hear you."
"I understand how hard this is for you."
"I'm glad to be with you."
"I can do something about what you are going through."

For example, I might pray something like, "Father, I had a hard day today. I feel like I failed at a task I was supposed to complete today and I've been feeling bummed about it all day."

In response, as I imagine how God might answer me, I might write, "My child, I see you curled up on your couch, tired and weary from your day. I see how much you wanted to complete the task and complete it well. I saw how you worked hard, but everything seemed to work against you. I see the heaviness in your heart and the disappointment you feel in yourself.

"I hear you telling yourself that you're a failure that you messed up. I hear your thoughts of worry as you wonder how this will affect your job or your review.

"I understand how hard this is for you, how you struggle to balance home and work life. I understand how much you want to get things perfect and how disappointed you feel when the results don't match your expectations.

REFERENCE

"I'm glad to be with you right now. I'm glad you brought your heavy heart and disappointment to me. I'm glad you're letting me meet you in this place of pain instead of running away."

"I can help you through this disappointment. You are a hard worker and did the best you could today despite all the setbacks. I am proud of you for all you accomplished today. It makes me so glad to see you using the skills I placed inside you."

The last step is to share what God is saying to each other. This is important because as the kids are getting to know God and his character, they will be uncertain if they are really hearing God's voice or if they're making it up. As they learn about God's character, and as they hear how God is speaking to the other children, their confidence will increase because they'll better understand God, who He is, and how He speaks to us. This will also help their relationships and trust with each other grow.

Group Prayer - This prayer method invites the kids to overcome their self-consciousness and get out of themselves to see they aren't the only ones who have things going on in their lives. It also helps them practice praying out loud.

Modified Sozo - The last two units in this book use a prayer method called Sozo. This is typically used in Inner Healing, however I've taken one very simple, and basic aspect of this to help the kids hear God's voice. The idea is to ask the three persons of God questions about how He sees us, and feels about us and vice versa. We can ask God to show us how we view Him. For example, we could ask God the Father to show us how He feels about us right now, or how He felt about us when we were performing a certain task. We could also ask the Holy Spirit and Jesus the same questions. Sometimes the kids will get a sense of something. An emotion will rise up in them, or a memory will pop up of them sitting in nature in a quiet place and the peaceful feeling that came with it. They might also get an image in their mind.

Service Project Ideas

Military Cards & Care Packages

www.operationgratitude.com has information on sending cards and care packages. They have lists for donations you can print out. This organization is on the BBB list of accredited charities.

www.packagesfromhome.com is another BBB accredited charity where you can send packages and letters. They also have lists of what is needed and where to send packages on their website.

REFERENCE

Operation Christmas Child

Many churches participate in this organization every year. If your church is one of them, have families bring donated items to the church and let the kids pack the boxes.

If your church doesn't participate in this, but you would like your students to, visit http://www.samaritanspurse.org/what-we-do/operation-christmas-child to print out flyers, donation lists, where to send the shoe boxes or find drop off locations near you, and a lot of other great information.

Compassion International

Compassion International is another great organization to get involved with. If you have enough interest shown, you can have your class raise money through tithes and offerings to sponsor a child.

If this seems too overwhelming, you can also collect funds for the Unsponsored Children's Fund. This collects donations for all the children who haven't been sponsored yet so they also get the things they need. This option can be a once a year event instead of an every month event.

Visit Compassion.com for more information on sponsoring a child.

For more information about the Unsponsored Children's Fund visit: http://www.compassion.com/church-engagement/child-help.htm

There is also an option for raising money for clean water. You can find that here: http://www.compassion.com/church-engagement/water-aid.htm

Helping the Homeless

There are a lot of things you can do to help the homeless.
1. You can collect food for your local food bank.
2. Find out if your local shelters accept homeless kits and have the kids put together packets of toiletries.
3. Collect warm clothes to donate to the homeless.
4. Collect board games for the homeless shelters.

REFERENCE

Other Service Project Ideas

1. Collect items for shelter animals.
2. Valentine's Cards for Senior Citizens.
3. Collect School Supplies for Kids in Need.
4. Collect old DVD's and games for a children's hospital.
5. Donate gently used stuffed animals to Police or Fire Departments for children in emergencies.

www.ingramcontent.com/pod-product-compliance
Lightning Source LLC
Chambersburg PA
CBHW060421010526
44118CB00017B/2300